#InThisTogether

Ministry in Times of Crisis

Curtis Ramsey-Lucas
Editor

JUDSON PRESS
PUBLISHERS SINCE 1824
VALLEY FORGE, PA

#InThisTogether: Ministry in Times of Crisis
© 2020 by Judson Press, Valley Forge, PA 19482-0851
All rights reserved.

Judson Press has made every effort to trace the ownership of all quotes. In the
event of a question arising from the use of a quote, we regret any error made
and will be pleased to make the necessary correction in future printings and edi-
tions of this book.

Bible quotations in this volume are from the New Revised Standard Version of
the Bible, copyright © 1989 by the Division of Christian Education of the National Council of the Churches of Christ in the United States of America. Used
by permission. All rights reserved.

Other scripture references are from the Contemporary English Version. Copyright
© 1991, 1992, 1995 by American Bible Society. Used by permission. The Message. Copyright © 1993, 1994, 1995. Used by permission of NavPress Publishing
Group. The New American Standard Bible, © 1960, 1962, 1963, 1968, 1971,
1972, 1973, 1975, 1977 by The Lockman Foundation. Used by permission. The
HOLY BIBLE, New International Version®, NIV®, copyright © 1973, 1978,
1984, 2011 by Biblica Inc. Used by permission. All rights reserved worldwide.
The *Holy Bible*, New Living Translation, copyright © 1996. Used by permission
of Tyndale House Publishers, Inc., Wheaton, IL 60189. All rights reserved.

Interior and cover design by Wendy Ronga, Hampton Design Group.

Library of Congress Control Number: 2020942729

Printed in the U.S.A.
First printing, 2020.

For Carol, with love

Contents

Contents

Introduction
The Crisis That Led to This Book

Curtis Ramsey-Lucas

> *"What our society looks like after this crisis depends on our collective understanding of the threats posed by inequity—and the work we do to address them."* —Timothy Shriver[1]

The first week of March 2020, I was making final edits and scheduling articles to be published in *The Christian Citizen* the following week. Several stories focused on Lenten practices while others recognized the observance of Women's History Month. I was also making plans to attend the American Association of People with Disabilities (AAPD) annual leadership awards gala in Washington, DC, where Senator Robert Dole was to receive an award.

That was before the novel coronavirus in the United States took a deadly turn, when in the span of just over a week, ten people died of COVID-19 in King County, Washington. On March 4, *The Christian Citizen* published a firsthand account of the situation in Kirkland, Washington, location of the first fatality from COVID-19 in the United States. In the weeks and months that followed, we published an extensive series of articles on ministry responses to COVID-19. Our writers stepped up to offer ideas for ensuring ministry continuity as churches shifted to online forms of gathering, tips and practices for clergy self-care, and how to engage in pastoral care in a time of self-isolation and social distancing.

Like many others, I spent the first months of the pandemic juggling working from home with online learning for children whose schools were closed, including my eldest, suddenly home from his final semester of college and facing the prospect of no graduation ceremony and an economy in free fall. My church, like so many others, moved worship services and prayer and study opportunities online and began to plan for the prospect of an extended period of ministry and pastoral care absent personal proximity. My employer, American Baptist Home Mission Societies, instructed all staff to work remotely and suspended onsite meetings at its Leadership and Mission Building in King of Prussia, Pennsylvania. Like so many others in workplaces and schools, we were soon all connecting and collaborating via Zoom.

In April, I asked *Christian Citizen* contributors to begin to consider the longer-term implications of the coronavirus crisis not only for the church but also for society—to begin to think of the days we are living through as an *apocalypse*, not in the popular understanding of that term as the end of history, but in the original Greek meaning of the term as a revelation, unveiling, or unfolding of things not previously known and which could not have been known apart from the unveiling. Specifically, I asked, what is this pandemic revealing about inequities and injustices in US society? What is it unveiling about the church? What good and evil is it unfolding? What hope is to be found in these times?

This led to a series of articles about the disproportionate impact of COVID-19 on African Americans in particular, and more generally on poor and vulnerable populations, due to disparities in access to health care and economic opportunity—disparities rooted in systemic racism and structural injustice. Our writers considered particular strengths of Baptist tradition and polity for approaching ministry in these challenging times, how life as we know it has fundamentally changed, and what needs to be different once life begins to return to something resembling "normal." Looking to the future, our writers warned of a rising tide of mental health concerns and the growing need for communities of faith to provide space for healing as individuals process grief.

During the time this second round of COVID-19 related articles was being published, George Floyd's very public death beneath the knee of Officer Derek Chauvin in Minneapolis sparked protests throughout the United States and around the world and furthered support for Black Lives Matter and other efforts to address historic, institutionalized racism in society. Floyd's death drew attention to further disparities and

injustices in the treatment of African Americans, including disproportionate rates of imprisonment, involvement with the criminal justice system, and mistreatment and death at the hands of police. Once again,
The Christian Citizen pivoted to cover this story including a firsthand
account of the Capitol Hill Occupied Protest in Seattle, why Americans
interpret current events in such divergent and divided ways, and what
hope can be found amid current division and unrest.

#InThisTogether

This volume collects some of these stories and more. Included are ex-
panded versions of articles previously published in *The Christian Citizen*,
as well as new content from ministry practitioners and subject matter
experts on ministry in times of crisis. Content is organized in five sec-
tions, each of which is framed by a broad question about what is being
revealed to us in these times of crisis:

- What We Learned About God
- What We Learned About Self
- What We Learned About Being Church
- What We Learned About Being Neighbors
- What We Learned About Our Nation

Each author writes from a perspective of Christian faith seeking understanding during the trials and tribulations of early twenty-first century
life in the United States. Our hope is that *#InThisTogether: Ministry in
Times of Crisis* will prompt further reflection and additional questions
that bear consideration in a variety of ministry contexts, and that it will
help inform your own approach to ministry in times of crisis.

From Krisis to Crisis

The word *crisis*, which is nearly identical to the Greek *krisis*, found its
way into the English language by way of Latin and French. In current
usage the word has a negative connotation and is a near synonym of

disaster or impending disaster, whereas the original Greek *krisis* meant judgment, result of a trial, selection. The root of *krisis* is *krei-*, a Proto-Indo-European word meaning to sieve, discriminate or distinguish.[2] In classical Greek, *krisis* was used to reference a dispute, a lawsuit, and a judgment about a lawsuit. In later English usage, the term was adopted as a medical reference to connote a decisive or critical point in the progress of an illness or disease. The course of two millennia of history and its usage in multiple and distinct cultures has resulted in its meaning undergoing significant alteration. Common contemporary usage denotes any bad situation which is urgent to some degree such as environmental crisis, political crisis, economic crisis, or crisis of faith.

In its original meaning, *crisis* implied judgment, a situation calling for choice and decision, and, according to Christian understanding, for discerning the will of God and the courage to follow it. We would do well to recapture this meaning of the word in the context of ministry in times of crisis, to be reminded that crisis has a deeper meaning than impending disaster or a bad situation which is urgent to some degree. As Alexander Schmemann wrote, "It is always good for the Church to be reminded by God that 'this world,' even when it calls itself Christian, is in fact at odds with Gospel of Christ, and that 'crisis' and the tension created by it are, after all, the only 'normal' mode of the Church's relationship with the world, with *any* world."[3]

None of Us Walks Alone

The AAPD gala convened as planned in March, though I did not attend. As in years past, emerging disability rights activists were recognized, and awards were given to corporate and political leaders. Dole received AAPD's Lifetime Impact Award. From his first speech as a United States Senator in 1969, to his return to the Senate chamber in 2014, to support the adoption of the UN Convention on the Rights of Persons with Disabilities, Dole has championed equal access and opportunity for people with disabilities. He also played a key role in passage of the Americans with Disabilities Act, landmark legislation that became law thirty years ago, in July 1990.

"We all face challenges in life—some have a tougher road than others," Dole wrote in a letter accepting the award. "But what sets us apart is how each one of us chooses to handle those challenges. Our resilience. I've faced a few bumps in the road throughout my life, but I've always tried to maintain a sense of optimism—looking ahead at brighter days to come.[4]

Through the bumps in the road, the crises of life, what sets us apart is how we *choose* to handle those challenges.

Looking ahead, amid this pandemic and the injustices and inequities it has revealed, I appreciate Dole's words. The road we have traveled thus far has been rough. There will be further bumps along the way. Our resilience—as individuals, communities, and as a nation—will continue to be tested. How will we respond? How will we choose to handle the crises we face? Will we struggle to maintain a sense of optimism? Will we remain hopeful or give ourselves over to despair? Will we manage to keep our eyes fixed on brighter days to come?

"None of us walks the path of life alone," Dole wrote in the closing of his letter. "We help each other along the way." Truly we are in this together. That fact has seldom been more apparent even as we struggle to reconcile its implications and wrestle with the challenges of moving forward united amid deep rooted injustice and political and cultural divisions.

Notes

1. Timothy Shriver, "Isolation Isn't New for Those with Intellectual Disabilities," *The Washington Post*, May 14, 2020.

2. *The American Heritage Dictionary of the English Language*, 5th ed. (2020), s.v. "crisis."

3. Alexander Schmemann, *Church, World, Mission* (Crestwood, NY: St. Vladimir's Seminary Press, 1979), 10.

4. For the full text of Dole's letter, see: Curtis Ramsey-Lucas, "'None of Us Walks the Path of Life Alone'—Sen. Robert Dole's Message to the Disability Community is What We All Need Right Now," The Christian Citizen, March 19, 2020, https://christiancitizen.us/none-of-us-walks-the-path-of-life-alone-sen-robert-doles-message-to-the-disability-community-is-what-we-all-need-right-now/.

SECTION ONE

What We Learned About God

1
The God Who Heals amid Crises
Debora Jackson

The traditional Sunday school curriculum teaches us from an early age that God is omniscient, omnipotent, and omnipresent. Because our human capacity cannot fully capture all that God is, our pedagogical practices ascribe states of being to God as a way of understanding our Creator. We note that God is all knowing, God is all powerful, and God is present with us in all things. We also learn that God is holy, meaning that God is set apart, and to be held in awe as perfect and transcendent, which is why we worship God. We learn that God is unchanging the same yesterday, today, and tomorrow. It is that quality of immutability that asserts God's unchanging nature, while upholding the assurance of God's covenantal promises.

These are the rational, cognitive ways of knowing God, but such epistemologies do not serve during a crisis. During crisis, we need a personal God who sees us in our suffering and cares about our condition. The good news is we have such a personal God. In Exodus 3, when Moses encountered God through the bush that burned but was not consumed, the LORD referred to God's self by three different names. God is Elohim, which is a generic name given to gods. God is LORD or Yahweh meaning "the Eternal," which is God's own personal name according to Torah. And God is "Ehyeh-Asher-Ehyeh." God uses this name when Moses asked, "Who should I say sent me?" Ehyeh means, "I am" or "I will be." Asher could mean "who" or "what." The second occurrence of Ehyeh could mean "I am" or it could suggest a future tense, that is "I will be." Most commentators have understood both occurrences of Ehyeh to convey the future tense and to mean: "I will be what tomorrow demands."[1]

Such a name identifies a personal God who cares about humanity and reminds us of how God shows God's self in history. For example, in Genesis 16, a pregnant and abused Hagar encountered the angel of the LORD who affirmed that God knew of her afflictions. Hagar named the LORD who spoke to her El Roi. She praised the God who sees, for God had seen her plight and given heed to her affliction.[2] Her personal experience enabled her to recognize the God whom she needed in that moment.

Abraham also encountered this personal God when he, in obedience to God's command, prepared to sacrifice his son Isaac (Genesis 22). Before Abraham could take Isaac's life, the angel of the LORD stopped him and God provided a ram, whose horns were caught in a thicket, to be used as sacrifice instead of his son. According to the traditional transliteration of the too-holy-to-write name for God, Abraham named the place Jehovah Jireh, which literally means "the Eternal will see," or as the New Revised Standard Version of the Bible suggests, "The LORD will provide."

God as provider was the God that I knew through the Black church. This God made a way out of no way. God exalted the valleys and made hills and mountains low. God made the first the last and the last the first. This God, as the old prayers intoned, was "A doctor in the sickroom, a lawyer in the courtroom, a mother to the motherless, and a shelter in the time of storm." And amid crisis, this personal God is the God who heals.

Our Scriptures affirm this is God's ultimate desire for humanity. In Ephesians 2, Paul explains that even though we were dead because of sin and living according to our human desires, God made us alive through Jesus Christ by God's grace and love. Through Jesus Christ, God healed the enmity between God's self and humanity. In short, the God who provides gave us what we needed, which was restoration in and reconciliation to God through Jesus Christ. However, God's desire to heal and reconcile humanity continues, and I have come to appreciate three such means of healing during a crisis.

First, God wants to heal our understanding of God's sovereignty. As the psalmist said, "The earth is the LORD's and all that is in it, the world, and those who live in it" (Psalm 24:1). God is the Creator of all and everything belongs to God. God asserts this in Exodus 20:2-3. In fact, the words "'I am the LORD your God' is an affirmative declaration of the dominion of the Almighty over the universe and [God's] authority as the Lawgiver."[3] Such recognition moved ancient Jewish historians Philo and Josephus to regard the directive, "I the Eternal am your God... You shall have no other gods before me," as the first commandment.[4] Therefore, we must understand and accept God's sovereignty, for God is ultimate and eternal. When we understand God's sovereignty as a commandment, we understand why violation is so significant. To allow other gods to supplant God is tantamount to rejecting God's sovereignty.

Of course, we might take exception to the charge that we are placing other gods before God, as few in our Western Christian society are carving graven images or erecting Asherah poles. But we have our gods. For example, consider the consuming and encompassing impact of digital technology on our lives. Studies suggest that regular workdays are extended, and people remain tied to the world of work beyond a base schedule, because mobile devices create a permanent contact with the affairs of the organization.[5] The result is an inability to turn off and create necessary psychological detachment from work. Technology also dominates our personal lives. Adults in the United States spent about three hours and thirty minutes a day using the internet in 2019, and the overall time Americans spend on various media is expected to grow to nearly eleven hours per day in 2020.[6] The apostle Paul encourages us to maintain a constant state of fellowship and connection with God through prayer. (1 Thessalonians 5:16-18). However, when our days are consumed predominantly by other matters, be they work or media, we must confront the possibility that those matters have become our gods.

But the crisis of a worldwide pandemic changed things, and God reasserted God's sovereignty over any other gods we had erected. Let me be clear: as sovereign, God can use whatever means desired to effect God's plan and purpose. Thus, far from suggesting that God brought about the pandemic, I believe God used a pandemic to draw people to God's self. History will record that the United States effectively shut down in March 2020. Businesses, schools, governments, and social events were halted because of the novel coronavirus, which none had ever seen and for which there was no cure. Schools closed, leaving students homebound. Retail and entertainment sectors closed, eliminating social outlets. Millions lost their jobs. We were advised, and in some places mandated, to shelter in place. Confined to our homes, estranged from community, and left with no other place to turn, we asked, "Why is this happening?" and "What does this mean?"

These are the questions that lead us to God, because these types of questions help us make sense of our experiences and enable us to orient ourselves toward some ultimate ideal.[7] It is an exercise of spiritual practice in which we are forced to confront the Eternal. Like Job, we questioned whether God had forsaken us. Like the prophet Habakkuk, we stationed ourselves on a rampart and awaited response. (Habakkuk 2:1). As we asked "Why?" we had the temerity to believe that we initiated contact with God, but our sovereign God was the initiator. The solitude of our circumstances led us to God, which was God's intent all along.

Second, having healed our understanding of God's sovereignty, God wants to heal our understanding of God's telos, or ultimate purpose. We read in Colossians 1:19-20 "For in him [Jesus Christ] all the fullness of God was pleased to dwell, and through him God was pleased to reconcile to [God's self] all things, whether on earth or in heaven, by making peace through the blood of his cross." This was God's atoning work and purpose: to reconcile humanity to God's self. Moreover, it was necessary. Because of sin, we were separated from God. As Isaiah 59:2 affirms, "Your iniquities have been barriers between you and your God, and your sins have hidden [God's] face from you so that [God] does not hear." Thus, humanity needed a healer. We needed that perfect sacrifice to sponge away the guilt and stain of sin for all time. Jesus Christ was the Lamb of God who was slain for our sins. His death was an act of sacrifice through which we could be saved. The result of this reconciling work was universal peace—both in heaven and on earth.[8]

It is this peace that is extended to us eternally by God and is not predicated upon individual acceptance. This point is important because it reinforces God's healing desire, which is most evident in crisis. Amid the coronavirus pandemic, for instance, some faith leaders asserted that COVID-19 was evidence of God's judgment.[9] But such presumption negates the offer of peace and reconciliation that God extended to humanity through Jesus Christ. Through the cross, Christ forever put to death the hostility that separated us from God. This means, especially in times of crisis, that God longs to heal not punish. God longs to save not condemn. To suggest that God's intent toward humanity during a crisis is punitive is to suggest that enmity remains. However, this is not the case, for the hostility between God and humanity due to sin was crucified on the cross. Especially in moments of crisis, I believe we can hear the words of God as spoken through Jesus in Matthew 23:37, "How often have I desired to gather your children together as a hen gathers her brood under her wings…" God has extended to us the gracious gift of reconciliation. Thus, as God promised, "Everyone who calls on the name of the Lord shall be saved" (Acts 2:21).

It is in this reconciling, saving grace of God that reminds us of a third aspect of God's desired healing: God wants to heal our understanding of God's penchant for the poor and the marginalized. Consider the person of Jesus. Jesus was a Jew in Roman-occupied Palestine, which was conquered in 63 BCE and governed by Herod the Great, a biracial Jew who ruled Judea as a Roman surrogate. Jesus grew up as an oppressed minority—oppressed not only by Rome, but also by the Jewish ruling class and the priestly aristocracy of Jerusalem. Socially, Jesus was of low standing, which seemed to be a source of embarrassment for New Testament authors. "Matthew changes the line to read not that Jesus was a carpenter but that he was a 'son of a carpenter.'"[10] And economically, Jesus was born into poverty, a fact made evident during Jesus' dedication at the temple when Mary offered two turtledoves as sacrifice; according to Leviticus 12:8, "If [the mother] cannot afford a sheep, she shall take two turtledoves or two pigeons, one for a burnt offering and the other for a sin offering."

Jesus fully embodied all that it meant to be oppressed and marginalized. And he emerged as a Savior with a penchant for the poor. It was their cause that Jesus championed when he declared the fulfilment of

Isaiah's prophesy in Luke 4:18, "The Spirit of the Lord is upon me, because he has anointed me to bring good news to the poor. He has sent me to proclaim release to the captives and recovery of sight to the blind, to let the oppressed go free, to proclaim the year of the Lord's favor." Entering humanity as an outcast born in a lowly manger, Jesus came to serve as messianic hero, righting the wrongs of the world and inverting systems that sought to privilege the powerful. Thus, "Jesus liberates us from the crushing burden of otherness and difference, bringing to light the God in us."[11] So, rather than seeing themselves as other and estranged, all who are marginalized are empowered through Christ to embrace a perspective that insists on their full acceptance as people made in the image of God. These truths demonstrate that Jesus' existence and example was about the restoration of humanity.

Asserting this point is critical in times of crisis because those who are oppressed and marginalized need healing. In April 2020, during the height of the novel coronavirus pandemic, the US unemployment rate rose to historic levels. Although the impact was widespread, people of color and women, who are among the most economically oppressed and marginalized, suffered the greatest losses. Hispanics and African Americans had higher unemployment rates than whites, and women were more likely than men to have lost their jobs.[12] The health impact of the disease was more dire for marginalized populations as well. African Americans and Latinos developed COVID-19 infections more frequently and died at disproportionate rates, demonstrating deeply entrenched healthcare disparities. Elderly people also died at higher rates than younger people from the disease. Then, in the midst of the health crisis, racial tensions reached a breaking point after the highly publicized death of three African Americans. Ahmaud Arbery was fatally shot by a white man while jogging. Breonna Taylor, an emergency medical technician, died from gunshot wounds sustained when police entered her home using a no-knock warrant. And George Floyd died after a police officer pinned Floyd to the ground and pressed his knee into Floyd's neck for eight minutes and forty-six seconds.

I believe that God has used, and will continue to use, these disparities and atrocities to demonstrate God's concern for those who are oppressed and marginalized. God needed humanity to see anew the precarious and perilous condition of those on the margins. Jesus told his disciples that "you always have the poor with you" (Matthew 26:11) and that truth has blinded society to their condition. But when millions lost their jobs and the majority of the unemployed were minorities, society was forced to confront the disparity. Too many who were already vulnerable were now facing severe hardship. People who were regarded as middle class were now experiencing food and housing insecurities. The plight of the unemployed forced elected officials across the political spectrum to come together, approving trillions of dollars of funding to help meet the needs of the hurting masses. God's desire to heal became society's collective desire as well.

However, the most hopeful sign of humanity's desire for global healing was in response to George Floyd's death. Protests occurred in all fifty states, attended by people of all ethnicities, ages, and socioeconomic backgrounds. Moreover, protests spread across the globe as people united in solidarity against police brutality, asserting what God has already affirmed: Black lives matter. The unity of Pentecost, when the Holy Spirit enabled people of all nations to understand the praising of God in their own languages, was made manifest in protest.

A crisis serves to sharpen what we already know about God. What may have started as a theoretical or rational understanding of God becomes personalized as a direct result of a crisis. This transformation heals our understanding of God as it moves us from head to heart. With a healed understanding, we recognize a sovereign God who can use crises to draw humanity to God's self. With a healed understanding, we experience God's ultimate purpose: to extend peace and reconciliation through Jesus Christ, not punitive punishments. And with a healed understanding, we recognize both that God is in solidarity with the poor and oppressed, and that God heals us by likewise moving our hearts to serve and support the poor. In moments of crisis, we are reminded that God wants to heal, for healing is what tomorrow requires.

Notes

1. W. Gunther Plaut and David E. S. Stein, eds., *The Torah: A Modern Commentary,* rev. ed. (New York, NY: Union for Reform Judaism, 2005), 364.

2. Debora Jackson, *Meant for Good: Fundamentals in Womanist Leadership* (Valley Forge, PA: Judson Press, 2019), 56.

3. Leo Michel Abrami, The Ten Commandments as Positive Affirmations, Jewish Bible Quarterly, Volume 38, No. 1, January 2010, https://www.questi-aschool.com/read/1G1-225793250/the-ten-commandments-as-positive-affirma tions, 3.

4. Plaut and Stein, *The Torah: A Modern Commentary*, 487.

5. Juan Sandoval-Reyes, Julio C. Acosta-Prado, Carlos Sanchís-Pedregosa, C. (2019). Relationship Amongst Technology Use, Work Overload, and Psychological Detachment from Work. *International journal of environmental research and public health*, 16(23), 4602. https://doi.org/10.3390 /ijerph16234602.

6. Rani Molla, "Tech Companies Tried to Help Us Spend Less Time on Our Phones. It Didn't Work," *Vox,* January 6, 2020, https://www.vox.com/recode /2020/1/6/21048116/tech-companies-time-well-spent-mobile-phone-usage-data.

7. Debora Jackson, *Spiritual Practices for Effective Leadership: 7Rs of Sanctuary for Pastors* (Valley Forge, PA: Judson Press, 2015), 40.

8. Arland J. Hultgren, "Christ the King, Year C," *The Lectionary Commentary: Theological Exegesis for Sunday's Texts, The Second Readings: Acts and the Epistles*, ed. Roger E. Van Harn (Grand Rapids, MI: Eerdmans Publishing Co., 2001), 337.

9. For example: In an interview, John Piper stated, "God can and does use illnesses to bring judgment sometimes upon those who reject him and his way." Desiring God, "How Do We Make Sense of the Coronavirus?" February 28, 2020, in *Ask Pastor John*, podcast, https://www.desiringgod.org/interviews/how-do-we-make-sense-of-the-coronavirus. A prominent church in Texas erected a billboard reading, "Is the coronavirus a judgment from God?" Jim Denison, "COVID-19 is Not God's Judgment" *Christianity Today*, April 21, 2020, https://www.christianitytoday.com/ct/2020/april-web-only/covid-19-is-not-gods-judgment.html.

10. Edward Collins Vacek, "Inquiring After God in Our Work," in *Inquiring After God: Classic and Contemporary Readings,* ed. Ellen T. Charry (Malden, MA: Blackwell Publishers, 2000), 92.

11. James H. Evans Jr., *We Have Been Believers, An African American Systematic Theology*, (Minneapolis: Fortress Press, 1992), 97–98.

12. Heather Long and Andrew Van Dam, "U.S. Unemployment Rate Soars to 14.7 Percent, the Worst Since the Depression Era," *Washington Post*, May 8, 2020, https://www.washingtonpost.com/business/2020/05/08/april-2020-jobs-report/.

2
God Is Not Sheltered in Place

Susan Sparks

While many of us—most of us—were sheltered in our homes, life became an ongoing contest to stay connected (and sane). A favorite diversion for me in the early days of the pandemic was the YouTube site "ZooBorns" that features fuzzy, newborn zoo animals.[1] During the week I wrote the original version of this article, the stars of the show were baby otters from Australia.

When sheltered in place, we are in a constant fight to keep our momentum, to keep our hearts buoyed, and to keep our sense of belonging and community. Even the smallest things can affect it, such as staying in your pajamas too long. While it's tempting to drape a colorful scarf over your cowgirl pajamas to field a conference call (or so I've heard), it may not be the best long-term plan.

According to an article in the *The Washington Post*, "going through an entire day in loungewear, it is easy to lose yourself and your sense of purpose and focus."[2] The article goes on to explain that getting dressed in the mornings "reminds us we are part of something." So, we get dressed and watch our newborn zoo animals, but there is still something significant missing. There's a hole in our hearts that can't be filled by wearing Calvin Klein or soothed by watching baby otters. It's a void that can only be filled by the One who never shelters in place: God.

If you have any doubt about this statement, spend thirty seconds flipping through one of the great ancient works of wisdom: the Bible.

■ I hereby command you: Be strong and courageous; do not be frightened or dismayed, for the LORD your God is with you wherever you go (Joshua 1:9).

- The LORD, your God, is in your midst (Zephaniah 3:17).
- I am with you always, to the end of the age (Matthew 28:20).

Notwithstanding the separation created by earthly walls, everyone is intimately connected through the presence of God. That is the common thread that holds our humanity together, a thread that will remain intact forever.

God is in our midst. And pandemic or not, the power of God surrounds us. The evidence is everywhere. All we have to do is look for it. For example, while surrounded by illness and infection, we in the Northern Hemisphere celebrated the first day of spring. To see evidence of this, all you had to do was look out your windows. Tiny yellow forsythias were starting to bloom. Brilliantly colored tulips were sprouting. Pigeons were doing embarrassingly intimate things on rooftops. Spring was springing.

Another website I watched during the early days of the pandemic was an eagle webcam in, of all places, Dollywood.[3] Unbeknownst to many, Dollywood has the largest exhibit of non-releasable bald eagles in the country, and in that sanctuary, tucked inside an eagle's nest, is a live webcam. Every day while I worked, I kept the webcam broadcast playing in the background.

As I wrote the article that formed the basis of this chapter, I watched the mother eagle, named Glenda by the sanctuary, use her wings to shelter a tiny, fuzzy, greyish fluffball that looked like an earmuff with claws. The fluffball, whom I affectionately named Sam, had his breakfast, pooped, and took a nap. Glenda snuggled sleeping Sam and nibbled on some dirt. My blood pressure was at an all-time low.

I was reminded of the many biblical images of eagles as guardians, such as "an eagle that stirs up its nest, and hovers over its young" (Deuteronomy 32:11). One of my favorite passages is Psalm 57:1: "Be merciful to me, O God, be merciful to me, for in you my soul takes refuge; in the shadow of your wings I will take refuge, until the destroying storms pass by." As I recalled that verse, I saw Sam peek out from under Glenda's wing. All you could see was his head; the rest of his body was nestled under hers, taking refuge, toasty and protected. Truly, that tiny eaglet had what every human being yearns for, longs for, aches for: to be safely surrounded by love, life, and belonging.

God—life—is not sheltered in place.

Every day, God bursts forth in our world, from a tiny eaglet in Tennessee, to the newborn ZooBorns in Australia, to the examples of human kindness bubbling up from the cracks and fissures of human life. From sheltered-in-place residents singing to each other across balconies in Italy,[4] to Canadians "caremongering"[5] for those in need, to two young cellists[6] who gave a concert on an elderly, homebound woman's porch, evidence of God's presence through human kindness can be found everywhere.

Scott Kelly, a retired NASA astronaut who spent a year isolated on the International Space Station noted how inescapably interconnected we are, and that the coronavirus has demonstrated that what we share is more powerful than what separates us. "One of the side effects of seeing Earth from the perspective of space," Kelly wrote, "is feeling more compassion for others. As helpless as we may feel stuck inside our homes, there are always things we can do."[7]

Consider the hospitals where healthcare workers risked their lives to save the lives of the COVID-19 patients in their care. Even there, hope shone forth. A nurse in our congregation shared that when a patient who had recovered from COVID-19 was released from the hospital, the song "Here Comes the Sun" was played as the patient departed. God's love also shone out in something as simple as choosing to wear a mask. The spread of COVID-19 was not attributable only to coughing, feverish people. It could also be spread by non-symptomatic people, both young and old. The simple choice of donning a mask indicated the wearer took seriously Jesus' words: "What you do to the least of them, you do to me."

How about wearing a mask and sharing joy? Wearing a mask doesn't mean you can't meaningfully connect with others. During the pandemic, my husband and I made an early morning trip to the Fairway Market on Second Avenue and Thirtieth Street in New York City every two weeks. While most people kept a fairly flat facial expression behind their masks, on one trip, a young woman looked up at us and smiled. Instinctively, both my husband and I smiled back at her. How do I know she smiled? Because she smized or smiled with her eyes. Louis Armstrong was right! Smile and "the whole world smiles with you."[8] Through her smile, the young woman in the market affirmed our deep connection as human beings, our holy connection that cannot be broken.

During the pandemic, God continued moving and stirring and empowering and healing and acting and listening—all while the physical doors of churches, synagogues, mosques, and other houses of worship throughout the world were closed. This was possible because God is not in the bricks of the temple, but in the hearts of the people. The Bible is full of stories and lessons that reinforce this important understanding of community. Consider the Exodus account of the Israelites wandering in the desert for forty years. Did God abandon them because they didn't have a permanent structure? No! As explained in Ezekiel 37:27, "My dwelling place shall be with them; and I will be their God, and they shall be my people."

Think about Jesus and the disciples. Did they worship, teach, or pray in a permanent structure? No. In fact, it was the opposite. They carried their ministry with them as they wandered Galilee, and God was with them every step of the way. What about the apostle Paul? While imprisoned alone in a cell, he wrote these words:

> You're no longer wandering exiles. This kingdom of faith is now your home country....God is building a home. He's using us all—irrespective of how we got here—in what he is building. He used the apostles and prophets for the foundation. Now he's using you, fitting you in brick by brick, stone by stone, with Christ Jesus as the cornerstone that holds all the parts together (Ephesians 2:19-22, THE MESSAGE).

We don't need a sanctuary, stained glass, or an organ to meet God. Hope, joy, life, and God spring forth without any such trappings. I can't help but think about the ending of Dr. Seuss's *How the Grinch Stole*

Christmas—specifically, the scene in which the Whos down in Whoville burst into song without the trappings of Christmas:

> "It came without ribbons! It came without tags!
> It came without packages, boxes or bags!"[9]

So, too, even in the midst of crises like a pandemic, the power of God—the power of hope, love, and compassion—bursts forth in our world. As the Whos might say, "It's here without steeples; it's here without pews; it's here without hymns, tiny Communion cups, or coffee-hour brews." In other words, we don't need a building to feel God's power. The attempt to "house" the Creator of the all things—including the Himalayas, the Orion Nebula, and an eaglet—is nothing short of pure arrogance.

The COVID-19 pandemic offered us a rare occasion for a second chance, an opportunity to look deep within, connect with the holy in our midst, and bring forth that light to fight for a better, healthier, more compassionate world. The award-winning author Arundhati Roy put it this way:

> Historically, pandemics have forced humans to break with the past and imagine their world anew. This one is no different. It is a portal, a gateway between one world and the next. We can choose to walk through it, dragging the carcasses of our prejudice and hatred, our avarice, our data banks and dead ideas, our dead rivers and smoky skies behind us. Or we can walk through lightly, with little luggage, ready to imagine another world. And ready to fight for it.[10]

Perhaps the most poignant example of God's presence that I witnessed in the pandemic came from within my own congregation. One of our newest babies, appropriately named Hope, was born in late December 2019 with a significant heart defect. She has survived two open-heart surgeries and numerous hospitalizations and procedures. Recently, her mom shared with me that in the midst of their family's unimaginable pain and fear, something remarkable happened: baby Hope learned to laugh.

To laugh. Within that little family, within our communities, within the nation, and within our troubled world, hope is springing forth. Joy is springing forth. Life is springing forth.

What will we tell our grandchildren, our great-nieces and -nephews, our young ones, when they ask, "What did you do during the great pandemic of 2020?" The children who experienced the pandemic will remember it. Maybe not every detail, but they will remember the big things—that birthday parties with their friends were cancelled, or that their grandparents couldn't visit, or that hugs were forbidden. What will we tell them we created from this pain? A return to business as usual? Or did we use this time of suffering to access and leverage the intimate power and presence of God to change our world? Two characters in J.R.R. Tolkien's *Lord of the Rings* framed it like this:

> "I wish it need not have happened in my time," said Frodo.
> "So do I," said Gandalf, "and so do all who live to see such times. But that is not for them to decide. All we have to decide is what to do with the time that is given us."[11]

Brothers and sisters, we are not alone in this time of crisis. We are never alone. For infused and permeated into every cell and microbe in this universe is the DNA, the presence, of the Creator. So, in your moments of crisis, be they personal, local, or global, get out of your pajamas and put on your clothes. Watch a few minutes of ZooBorns, then turn to the critical work at hand. Discover new ways to connect with those around you. Find ways to heal yourself and others. While we may be confined to our homes, the one who created us is not. Latch onto that life force. Channel that connection, and always remember:

God is not sheltered in place.

Notes

1. "ZooBorns," YouTube, https://www.youtube.com/user/ZooBorns.

2. Robin Givhan, "Our Clothes Tell Our Story. What Happens When the Narrative is Just Pajamas and Sweatpants?," *The Washington Post*, March 16, 2020, https://www.washingtonpost.com/lifestyle/2020/03/16/our-clothes-tell-our-story-what-happens-when-narrative-is-just-pajamas-sweats/.

3. "Dollywood Bald Eagle Nest Cams," American Eagle Foundation, https://dweaglecams.org/.

4. Vanessa Thorpe, "Balcony Singing in Solidarity Spreads Across Italy during Lockdown," *The Guardian*, March 14, 2020, https://www.theguardian.com/world/2020/mar/14/solidarity-balcony-singing-spreads-across-italy-during-lockdown.

5. Tom Gerken, "Coronavirus: Kind Canadians Start 'Caremongering' Trend," *BBC News*, March 16, 2020, https://www.bbc.com/news/world-us-canada-51915723.

6. Aila Slisco, "Watch the Viral Video of the Kids Who Put on a Cello Concert on Porch of Elderly Neighbor in Self-Isolation," *Newsweek*, March 16, 2020, https://www.newsweek.com/watch-viral-video-kids-who-put-cello-concert-porch-elderly-neighbor-self-isolation-1492643.

7. Scott Kelly, "I Spent a Year in Space, and I Have Tips on Isolation to Share," *The New York Times*, March 21, 2020, https://www.nytimes.com/2020/03/21/opinion/scott-kelly-coronavirus-isolation.html.

8. "When You're Smiling," written by Larry Shay, Mark Fisher and Joe Goodwin, 1928.

9. Theodor Seuss Geisel, *How the Grinch Stole Christmas* (New York: Random House, 1957).

10. Arundhati Roy, "The Pandemic is a Portal," *The Financial Times*, April 3, 2020, https://www.ft.com/content/10d8f5e8-74eb-11ea-95fe-fcd274e920ca.

11. J.R.R. Tolkien, *The Fellowship of the Ring* (New York: Houghton Mifflin Harcourt Publishing Co., 1954), 50.

3
Living Between Trapezes—Waiting in Uncertain Times
John Zehring

"And now, Lord, for what do I wait? My hope is in you"
(Psalm 39:7 NASB).

With the onset of the coronavirus pandemic, we found ourselves waiting in uncharted territory, the entire planet trapped between ordinary life and sheltering in place. It felt like we were living between trapezes. Having let go of the secure bar of the first trapeze, we hung in midair, awaiting the arrival of the next. But the next bar was not in sight. Epidemiologists and health professionals forecast a dramatic increase in infection rates and death. Non-essential businesses were forced to close. Unemployment reached levels not seen since the Great Depression. Churches and other houses of worship began gathering online.

Numerous articles and television segments offered suggestions for creative things to do while waiting but could not address our fundamental impatience with our new reality. A friend posted on Facebook at the time: "The truth is, it's not so boring at home. But it's interesting how one bag of rice has 7,456 grains and another has 7,489." For him, waiting was reduced to counting grains of rice. What else was he to do?

Who likes to wait, especially while mid-air between trapezes? You want to do something. Humans are naturally inclined to take action, to initiate, to do…even if it is the wrong thing. Indeed, the fifth book of the New Testament, a history of the early church, is not named the Book of Wait, but the Book of Acts. Many of us are not good at waiting. We want to see the ten-day forecast, the timeline, the strategic plan, the goal, and the expected outcomes. We scan the news constantly for data on the virus that might inform our decision-making. We want to see more of the map. We want a GPS to display a picture of the road to follow and a voice to tell us where to turn.

Waiting upon the Lord is not what we have in mind. Waiting feels passive and reactive. Acting feels proactive. And yet, our feelings are not always our best guide, for often our best course of action is to wait: "Wait for the LORD; be strong, and let your heart take courage; wait for the LORD!" (Psalm 27:14). People of faith have an advantage, for they have been schooled in waiting upon the Lord:

> "And now, LORD, for what do I wait? My hope is in you." (Psalm 39:7 NASB)
>
> "I wait for the LORD, my soul waits, and in his word I hope." (Psalm 130:5)

After Jesus' crucifixion, his disciples were living between trapezes. They wondered what they were supposed to do. Jesus answered that they were supposed to wait: "While staying with them, he ordered them not to leave Jerusalem, but to wait there for the promise of the Father" (Acts 1:4). Wait. That is probably not the answer the disciples hoped for. Waiting is not likely to pop into the forefront of your mind when facing anxiety. Just the opposite. It feels like you should be doing something.

Habakkuk did not know what to do and he was a prophet. He ought to have been able to advise people what to do and how to act in the times between trapeze bars. Habakkuk complained to God and went up on the ramparts of the city to wait for God to respond to his complaint. Ramparts are walls, like the wall surrounding a fortified city or the wall around a castle. What Habakkuk did when he didn't know what to do is something that you can use when you don't know what to do. Habakkuk needed direction, did not have a map, and so he went up to keep watch on the rampart and to wait upon the Lord. "I will take my stand at my watchpost, and station myself on the rampart; I will keep watch to see what he will say to me, and what he will answer concerning my complaint" (Habakkuk 2:1). Action is portrayed here not as providing the answers, but as waiting on God for them. Habakkuk continues, "Then the LORD answered me and said: Write the vision; make it plain on tablets, so that a runner may read it. For there is still a vision for the appointed time; it speaks of the end and does not lie. If it seems to tarry, wait for it; it will surely come; it will not delay. Look at the proud! Their spirit is not right in them, but the righteous live by their faith'" (Habakkuk 2:2-4). Again, wait. That is the take-home message. It is not a matter of having the answers, but of knowing how to wait upon God for them.

People of faith have experience waiting upon God. Adelaide A. Pollard captured this experience in her hymn, "Have Thine Own Way, Lord:"

> Have Thine own way, Lord! Have Thine own way!
> Thou art the potter, I am the clay.
> Mold me and make me after Thy will,
> While I am waiting, yielded and still.[1]

Adelaide Pollard was born in 1862 in Bloomfield, Iowa. She was named Sarah by her parents, but she did not like the name and later changed it to Adelaide. Pollard's life was not a success story, at least in her own mind. She taught at several girls' schools and for a while was a teacher at a missionary training school in Nyack, New York. But what she most wanted to do was go to Africa as a missionary. Her dream went unfulfilled. She tried and failed to raise the necessary funds; she made plans, and even went to Africa for a very short time, but she was unable to stay due to the outbreak of World War I. While once in a state of discouragement, Pollard attended a prayer meeting at her church where she heard a woman pray this simple prayer: "It really doesn't matter what you do with us, Lord. Just have your way with our lives." Inspired, Pollard went home and meditated on the woman's words and on texts that refer to God as the potter, including Jeremiah 18:3–4: "So I went down to the potter's house, and there he was working at his wheel. The vessel he was making of clay was spoiled in the potter's hand, and he reworked it into another vessel, as seemed good to him." Before going to bed that evening, Pollard wrote the stanzas of "Have Thine Own Way, Lord."[2]

Perhaps some of our greatest spiritual insights come out of what we perceive as our soul's distress. Who knows what spiritual growth or insights might emerge from our living between trapezes during the pandemic? When facing an uncertain future, remind yourself that waiting and trusting is frequently the best response. In so much of your life you have been taught to take initiative and to act. When between trapezes, learn that it is not completely up to you, but to you and God. Live by faith.

Waiting, or trusting in God, is well-portrayed in the beloved verse from Isaiah 40:31: "Those who wait for the LORD shall renew their strength, they shall mount up with wings like eagles, they shall run and not be weary, they shall walk and not faint." Those who wait for the Lord display the same intent as those who trust in God. To wait is to trust.

At my cottage on the coast of Maine, there is a tree where majestic American bald eagles land and sit for a while, keeping a watchful eye over the bay. They do not nest there but they visit often, swooping down to land on one of the tall pines' bare branches. My wife and I have been watching the eagles land and take off for a quarter century. We have watched them raise their young. We have heard their cries echo across the bay. We have been awakened by a family of eagles at five in the morning when they land in our tree. We can be sitting right next to the tree and an eagle will come and go as if we were not even there. The eagle lands in the tree with a flappy flutter. It sits there as it preens and primps itself. And then—you can see it coming—it starts to get restless, it twitches a bit, and, with a ceremonial *harrumph*, it leaps away from the branches, and climbs heavenward to the heights where it will soar.

Isaiah must have watched an eagle in a tree too, because he described the behavior perfectly when he used it as a metaphor for one of the greatest truths about God and about you. The Contemporary English Version translates the familiar and beloved verse, "Those who trust the Lord will find new strength" (Isaiah 40:31).

In times of crisis, we need new strength. Any major change in your life can cause stress. That is when a renewal of strength is especially treasured. So, we wait upon God as we pray "Mold me and make me after Thy will, While I am waiting, yielded and still."

Consider a story told about a trapeze artist who instructed his students how to perform on the high trapeze bar. After teaching what to do, he told them, "Now, get up there and demonstrate your ability." One student looked up at that insecure perch and froze. Struck with fear, he had a vision of falling to the ground. His fright was so deep, he could not move a muscle. "I can't do it!" he said. The instructor put his arm around the boy's shoulder and said, "Son, you can do it, and I will tell you how." Then he shared his trade secret. He said, "Throw your heart over the bar and your body will follow." His secret was to visualize.[3]

Stephen Covey wrote:

> You can visualize in every area of your life. Before a performance, a sales presentation, a difficult confrontation, or the daily challenge of meeting a goal, see it clearly, vividly, relentlessly, and over and over again. Create an internal 'comfort zone.' Then, when you get into the situation, it isn't foreign. It doesn't scare you.[4]

That's what we can do. We can visualize ourselves surviving, enduring, and perhaps even thriving as we live between trapezes. Psalm 23:4 poetically describes our credo: "Even though I walk through the darkest valley, I fear no evil; for you are with me." Note the word *through*. We walk *through* this dark valley. Visualize yourself walking through the valley, with the Good Shepherd accompanying you and leading you. You may not know how long the valley will be, but visualize yourself emerging from the other end. Dream it, because, as athletes typically attest, "If you can dream it, you can do it."

Throw your heart over the bar, visualize the successful conclusion to living between trapezes, and take inspiration from a quote attributed to the Roman poet Virgil: "He can conquer who believes he can." She can conquer who believes she can. When Beethoven was threatened with deafness he said: "I will take fate by the throat; it will never bend me completely to its will."[5] Booker T. Washington, in his autobiography *Up from Slavery*, wrote, "I have learned that success is to be measured not so much by the position that one has reached in life as by the obstacles which he has overcome while trying to succeed."[6]

Paul describes in Romans how people of faith can hang in there no matter what the circumstances: "We also boast in our sufferings, knowing that suffering produces endurance, and endurance produces character, and character produces hope, and hope does not disappoint us, because God's love has been poured into our hearts through the Holy Spirit that has been given to us" (Romans 5:3-5). The Revised Standard Version begins, "We rejoice in our sufferings..." That is enough to stop a person in their tracks. When it comes to suffering, rejoicing is not the first thing that comes to mind. If anything, we rejoice when we are not suffering or when suffering has passed by. But to rejoice in our suffering? That begs for an explanation, and Paul provides it.

Paul is addressing people of faith who have an attitude of possibility. People of faith suffer like anyone else. By becoming a Christian, a person does not escape the challenges that all people encounter. However, the person of faith possesses an attitude that changes how they see the difficulties. Paul details this in a letter to the Corinthians:

> We are afflicted in every way, but not crushed; perplexed, but not driven to despair; persecuted, but not forsaken; struck down, but not destroyed; always carrying in the body the death of Jesus, so that the life of Jesus may also be made visible in our bodies (2 Corinthians 4:8-10).

People of faith will not be crushed, will not be driven to despair, and will not be destroyed. People of faith recognize the bad but look to the good; acknowledge the darkness but bask in the light; grieve from loss but find comfort and strength beyond their own; and worry about what they see but hope in the unseen. Even when people of faith experience the worst, they cling to their trust that the best is yet to come, because God is good, all the time. All the time, God is good.

Suffering, Paul writes, produces endurance. The Greek word Paul used for endurance is *hupomone*, which means more than endurance. A good translation for *hupomone* is fortitude. Suffering produces an attitude of fortitude. *Hupomone* is the attitude that believes it can overcome. It is the spirit that does not passively endure but that actively overcomes the challenges and difficulties of life. *Hupomone* is the hope that everything in life can be used for God's glory and for personal betterment. Suffering produces an attitude of fortitude, and fortitude produces character, and character produces hope. Helen Keller, who lost both hearing and sight at a young age, captured one of the best definitions of *hupomone*, of fortitude. She said, "Although the world is full of suffering, it is also full of the overcoming of it."[7]

The psalmist wrote, "On the day I called, you answered me, you increased my strength of soul" (Psalm 138:3). The strength of a person's spirit has more to do with their ability to endure, to overcome suffering, or even thrive under adversity than anything else. Perhaps you have witnessed people of faith who faced insurmountable obstacles or heart-wrenching challenges who somehow remained strong and maintained a positive attitude. This is because of strength of soul. Pray it: "Dear God, I pray for you to increase my strength of soul."

There is an anonymous benediction that blesses with these words:

> Go from here with open arms, with head held high and with love in your heart. No matter what happens, always remember that you are beautiful and loved by God. Always believe in yourself. Go out and follow your dreams, and if your dreams go up in smoke, build new dreams and follow them. Grab hold of your future and change your world as Christ has changed

your life. Be everything you can be. Be at peace with your neighbor and your God and be happy.

A phrase that stands out is "Go out and follow your dreams, and if your dreams go up in smoke, build new dreams and follow them." People with an attitude of fortitude are not naïve. They are aware that dreams may not materialize, but they also possess a can-do spirit that has determined if their dreams go up in smoke, they will build new dreams. They know in their hearts and souls that suffering produces endurance, and endurance produces character, and character produces hope, and hope does not disappoint us.

Living between trapezes is not a choice we anticipate but, as people of faith, we shall face it with hope—waiting upon the Lord, trusting in God, throwing our heart over the bar, visualizing a successful outcome, and determining to face obstacles with God-given fortitude. We will go out and follow our dreams, and if our dreams go up in smoke, we will choose to build new dreams and follow them. Ultimately, we shall grab hold of our future and change our world as Christ has changed our life.

Notes

1. "Have Thine Own Way, Lord," Hymnary.org, https://hymnary.org/text/have_thine_own_way_lord.

2. "Sarah Pollard Didn't Like Her Name," ChristianityToday.com, last updated June 2007, https://www.christianity.com/church/church-history/timeline/1801-1900/sarah-pollard-didnt-like-her-name-11630530.html.

3. Adapted from Norman Vincent Peale, *The Power of Positive Thinking* (New York: Touchstone, 1952).

4. Stephen R. Covey, *The 7 Habits of Highly Effective People* (Simon & Schuster: New York, 1989), 134.

5. Maria Popova, "Take Fate by the Throat: Beethoven on Creative Vitality and Resilience in the Face of Suffering," *Brain Pickings*, https://www.brainpickings.org/2017/09/19/beethoven-take-fate-by-the-throat/.

6. Booker T. Washington, *Up From Slavery: An Autobiography* (Garden City, NY: Doubleday & Company, Inc.: 1900), 39.

7. Maria Popova, "Helen Keller on Optimism," *Brain Pickings*, https://www.brainpickings.org/2013/06/21/helen-keller-on-optimism/.

SECTION TWO

What We Learned
About Self

4

Lessons amid Disaster

Matthew Crebbin

For many reasons, I would rather not write what I am about to write. I do not want to know what I know, because I learned my lessons about disaster ministry from an ugly, horrific event, one that still resonates within my own soul, my local community, and our nation. On December 14, 2012, I sat in a fire station next to Sandy Hook Elementary School and was called forth to minister as my community suffered unimaginable devastation to heart, mind, body and soul. Twenty children and six adults had just been killed in one of the deadliest mass shootings in the United States. I was not trained to address anything like that in seminary.

My education in disaster ministry taught me some difficult lessons about trauma and ministry. Disasters are merciless teachers. Rarely do you have the time or the resources to respond as effectively or as transformatively as you would want. In addition, every tragedy is different. No community or individual experiences a calamity exactly the same. The trauma spreads and grows in ways that depend upon the nature of the event, the location of the disaster, and the unique circumstances surrounding the incident. I do not know how current or future disasters will be experienced by the specific community in which you minister. However, there are a few things I have learned that I wished someone had told me about ministry and trauma before I was overwhelmed by the wave the crashed over my life on that day in December. Hopefully some of these lessons will be helpful to you in the coming days, months, and years.

You Are Going to be a Hero. Don't Get Used to It

There will be all kinds of heroes in the early days of a disaster. And yes, all of them should be honored. So if you fulfill your role as a pastor in the midst of a disaster—if you care for your people, organize your community, and seek to respond to the exhaustive needs of the world around you—then many people will see you as a hero. Do not take it personally. Any hero worship you experience will have very little to do with you, and it probably will not last. During a crisis, people pull together, look fear, death, and horror in the face, and do the best they can to meet it with courage, compassion, and love. Disasters can produce feelings of hyper-connectedness in which people feel closer to one another. Differences, distinctions, and disagreements large or small can be overlooked in the name of a larger purpose. Indeed, some people, including pastors, might look back fondly upon the early days of a disaster as both an awful and idyllic time when everyone was finally a "real" community. Unfortunately, such times do not last. Do not fall for the temptation of idealizing others or yourself during those early days.

If you minister beyond those early moments of a disaster, you will also be a part of the natural grief that pulls people's lives apart and causes many to look for someone or something to be angry with. That someone or something might end up being you. Don't take that personally either. Disasters by their nature cause chaos that can be physical, emotional, spiritual, or any combination of those. Such chaos can only be kept at bay for a while. Ultimately, the journey out of a disaster will require people to face, integrate, and, hopefully, transform chaos into a new form of wisdom. Such a journey is rarely simple or easy, and many people will face the inadequacy of their personal and communal resources to deal with such overwhelming loss and grief.

You Are Going to Have a Hard Time Taking Care of Yourself

In the early days of a disaster, you will probably put off doing the things you know you need to do in order to be the best pastor and human being that you can be. Maybe you were the sort of person who did this even before the disaster. You might be tempted to make a bargain with yourself such as, "I'll do that tomorrow," or "I'll take care of myself and/or my most personal, intimate relationships when things are better in another week or another month." Or maybe you will think, "If I just make it another month," or "When a vaccine comes then I'll be able to…." In a disaster, the time you think you will have later never actually comes. In most disasters, there is no "better" or "normal" at the end of the journey. There is only a new reality that may continue to cause you and those around you to feel out of sorts. If you do not commit to self-care during a disaster and in the months and years afterwards, some part of you—body, mind and/or soul—will end up paying a high price for the neglect.

By definition, a disaster means that the resources of the community are overwhelmed. There is always more that you will be able to offer on the "altar of the good." If you are not careful, you will offer up your very self or the wellbeing of your family and other intimate relationships in the name of the overwhelming need around you. Of course, if you end up sacrificing self and loved ones, there will not be much left of you to serve as the transforming representative of God's love in the world. The "altar of the good" will willingly take anything and everything that you have to offer. Do not surrender to the temptation of believing that God needs your own personal destruction to save the world. It is not only bad personal self-care, it is bad public theology.

Focus More on Purpose than on Meaning

One of the mistakes many faith leaders make during and in the aftermath of a disaster is believing they have been called to make meaning out of the chaos. They are the local theologians after all. In general, making meaning out of the chaos is not what people need most. This is not to say that meaning is unimportant; it is simply to say that questions of theodicy may not be helpful to those who are actively struggling with a traumatic event. After the Sandy Hook shooting, the only people who asked me, "Where was God in the midst of this?" were reporters. People living with the chaos of a disaster do not have the energy required to get their heads around the "meaning of it all." What they desperately need is a purpose.

This was one small blessing in the early days of the COVID-19 pandemic: people were given a purpose. They were asked to practice physical distancing and to alter daily routines for the sake of a higher purpose—namely, reducing the spread of the disease. Of course, this came with great anxiety and grief, as well as real economic and physical hardship. Hopefully, you were able to affirm to your congregation that their physical distancing was a profound calling, a holy task of love.

One of the great opportunities you as a pastor have in a disaster is to help people in your community to find ways to make a difference. Every disaster is different, and so every response will require creativity. But most disasters do share some common needs even when the circumstances may be very different. Certain people in your community will need the basics— food and shelter—as well as other resources that are in short supply—connection, continuity, and inspiration. This is a starting point to use to use when determining what might be needed in a time of disaster as well as for determining how your community might find purpose in responding to such needs. It is why churches for many decades have had formal and informal "casserole brigades" for families who are sick or have lost loved ones. People feel powerless in the face of suffering and are not sure how to make meaning of a loss, but being able to bake a tuna casserole somehow helps the giver to find purpose in an intimate time of chaos. In a disaster you need to scale up the "casserole brigade" responses of your faith community. The COVID-19 pandemic found people sewing and donating face masks, providing food for hospital staffs, sending meals to sick families, and knitting prayer shawls for grieving loved ones.

One note of caution: Do not end up contributing to the "disaster within the disaster." Sometimes people do things in response to a disaster that they think will be helpful but instead end up stretching already critical resources even more. For example, after the Sandy Hook shooting, people from across the country sent thousands of stuffed animals. The toys filled up two Sunday school classrooms, and it was a real struggle to figure out what to do with them. So, use your creativity and good judgement, but do find ways to give people a purpose.

Use the Body to Calm the Mind

Trauma changes how the brain works. Prolonged anxiety and stress affect the brain in similar ways. To oversimply a very complex subject: The part of the brain called the amygdala activates the "fight or flight" response and stores emotional and threat-related memories. During times of bodily threat, the amygdala takes over and overwhelms other cognitive brain functions. This response enabled our ancient human ancestors to survive in a dangerous world. However, often when people experience trauma or sustained periods of stress and anxiety, the amygdala continues to be the driver of the brain instead of the prefrontal cortex. The prefrontal cortex is the part of the brain that regulates attention and awareness, makes decisions, determines meaning and emotional significance, and so on. If you have ever ministered to people around a time of death or loss, many of them will later tell you that they don't remember what you said to them. That is because their cognitive functioning had been compromised.

What does this mean for ministry during this time? First, do not assume people are going to be making good, thoughtful decisions. And do not take it personally when those people are in your church. Second, you are not going to help calm people by simply telling them to "be calm". You need to find ways to encourage people to use their bodies to calm their minds. There are many ways to do this: walking, yoga, tai chi, dancing, breathing techniques, meditation, prayer, and mindfulness training. If you are not already familiar with these and other such techniques, find more information. Using the body to calm the mind will be a long-term need within a community affected by a disaster. Our church has been offering yoga three times a week for many years now. The need does not end six months after a disaster. Such need may exist for years to come.

Be a Storyteller

While people are often not looking for the "meaning of it all" in the midst of trauma, they are aching for a sense of belonging. We humans have an innate desire for our own personal story be a part of a larger story. That is why we have been telling stories of all kinds around campfires and cathedrals for thousands of years. Remember, Israel wrote down and shared the stories of the Exodus struggle many years later while they were living in exile in Babylon. The story of Exodus is not pretty; it is filled with all kinds of human failure and folly. But it sustained a people during their time of dislocation. One of the things I noticed during the early days of the COVID-19 pandemic was an uptick in storytelling by all kinds of organizations using online platforms. We human beings often have good instincts about what we need.

This is one of the things faith communities have been doing from the beginning days of their traditions. They have been sharing a grand narrative about life and death, suffering and joy, despair and hope for centuries. The key in this moment is that you should not think you are called to offer only "and they lived happily ever after" versions of the narrative. The Christian faith story is filled with honest laments and frightful acts of horror. It tells of all kinds of people: some filled with fear, some filled with faith, and some filled with both at the same time. Many of our faith ancestors are remembered as liars and cheaters. Our story is often brutally honest about what it is like to be lost and then to be found. It pulls no punches about the ugliness or the beauty that is a part of our common humanity. Sometimes those in ministry are tempted to "clean up" the rough edges of our sacred story, especially during hard times. But disasters often require honest acceptance that our world can be an ugly and fearful place. Trauma is not defeated by oversimplified and sanitized storytelling. One of the greatest gifts of our ancient story is how improper any number of our faith stories are. You do not have to claim that people easily overcame hardship because they were righteous or that they transformed their circumstances because they were cleaver. Our faith stories remind us that even in the bleakest of our human moments, God's enduring love sustains. The story of faith is a story that affirms that hope and joy do not depend upon appearances to the contrary or the circumstances of the moment.

Beloved colleagues, share the story. Embrace all of it and allow it to speak the truth needed for this moment. Your communities need authentic storytellers who can help them experience what it is like to be held by something greater than their minds and hearts can comprehend in this moment. They need to know they are a part of a story that will hold them even in their most anxious moments or during their most bloodcurdling screams. When all else fails, simply remember: You are worthy of care. You have a purpose. Remember to breathe. And most of all remember: You, too, are loved.

5

Beyond Resilience—Self-Care to Build Fitness

Naomi Kohatsu Paget

This many years later, I still wonder how I slept so peacefully during some of the most terrifying nights imaginable. The 2011 earthquake was one of the strongest ever recorded in Japan and 29,000 people died. My colleagues and I had walked miles to assess the damage, needs, our resources, and whether they would be adequate. And we were dodging the threat of Fukushima's radiation leak. We met survivors with horrifying stories and saw the bodies of those who did not survive. And when I laid down that night, I fell into restful slumber.

Years later I would wonder if I had been in denial. Was it shock? Why could I manage such freedom from anxiety during such a physically, emotionally, and spiritually demanding time as that? After years of study, I am convinced it was self-care.

Self-care sounds selfish and narcissistic, although it is critical to the practice of ministry. It sounds like looking out for myself because I'm so important or because no one else will do it. I think there is some truth to that. If I'm going to be emotionally fit, I have a responsibility to do something about that fitness. Every one of my lectures has included the statement, "You can't give people what you do not have."

What We Know

Self-care is usually defined as an action that one takes to provide physical, emotional, relational, behavioral, mental, and spiritual well-being for oneself. Self-care is self-initiated and is under the individual's control. It's a lot like preventative medicine with the intention of avoiding emotional and physical distress in particular.

A recent Harris Poll reported that 44% of consumers believe self-care is only possible for people with discretionary time. It also reported that

35% believe it is possible only for those with enough money.[1] Many health providers suggest that incorporating healthy self-care practices into daily life don't have to be expensive or time-consuming to be effective. And still, many people have no intentional, regular touchstones for self-care.

Perfectionists and goal setters often mistake self-improvement for self-care. In time, we may have some similar results, but self-improvement usually has its reward in the future. Self-care provides an instant reward—a sense of calm, a moment of respite, a peaceful interval during the chaos of the situation and circumstances. Self-care is a present experience, but it also has future returns.

A High Calling and High Anxiety

To be called as a minister to those who are impacted by disasters and crises is a high calling. It is a calling that few receive as a specific and intentional call. The boundaries are clear and unforgiving. Those who answer it will almost always be providing ministry to the hurt, the lost, the misunderstood, the grieving, and the disenfranchised of the world. There will be few wedding celebrations, baby dedications, graduations, or holidays. Sometimes the best we can hope for is the joy of finding a treasured memento in the ashes of a home or the relief of learning that someone's home is still standing. Accepting a calling to disaster ministry is to accept the ministry of interruptions, the ministry of lament, and the ministry of presence. It is an intentional step into chaos, confusion, and distress.

Ministry during a crisis is filled with stress. Your eye wants to twitch and your breakfast tastes awful, again. Ministry in the aftermath of crisis is filled with grief—so many losses that survivors must face. There is the loss of a home, belongings, memorabilia, and things that can never be replaced. There's the loss of friends or loved ones or pets. There's the loss of your sense of safety and your sense of community. There's loss of order and loss of structure. There's so much grief and you must provide solace when only lamenting seems appropriate.

There is Very Little Margin in Our Overloaded Lives

Richard Swenson, MD, writes about what he terms *marginless* living.[2] Technology and progress have improved one part of our lives, and yet we seem to have less margin for other parts of our lives. We know more and we can get more done. The missing pieces seem to be that we don't relate as well, we are not emotionally fulfilled, and we even feel spiritually bankrupt sometimes. Progress has caused us pain and the only real answer is "margin." We must create margin in our overloaded lives.

Be Aware of Clergy Killers

We have ministered in the world of abuse, neglect, anger, unforgiveness, resentment, hopelessness, and evil. Any one of those issues could leave a sense of overwhelming loss. It sometimes feels like there's not enough energy and stamina to deal with the matters that erode our spirit.

Ministers in disasters will face some of the most difficult issues that people deal with every day. When we empathize with those feelings, we, too, are on the path of annihilation. Our own spirits can be destroyed by the abuse we see in others, the unforgiveness that torments people, and the hopelessness that drives people to suicide. Clergy killers are not necessarily people or viruses, guns or bombs. Clergy killers are often the difficult issues we face and feel so responsible to fix. We feel people's pain, we experience their loneliness, and we have a personal knowledge of grief from our own sense of not being able to fix all these problems.

What We Know That We Should Do

We Must Find a Timely Balance for Effective Ministry

Almost every article about health and well-being mentions finding balance in one's life. Time management studies are about finding balance in the amount of time one spends on each aspect of the day, week, month, and year. Research "finding peace" and you will find the mention of balance. This equilibrium we are all seeking to establish is limited by each context. What feels like balance during a lazy afternoon is nothing like the balance we need while taking refuge in a tornado shelter or surgical waiting room.

Most people try to allot specific amounts of time to their day to find balance—one hour in prayer and devotions, four hours with the family, six hours in direct ministry with people, two hours in research and study, one hour administrative duties, one hour managing people, one hour community service, one hour ministry of interruptions, one hour maintenance of home or office or church or something, and lest I forget, eight hours for sleep and personal maintenance. Wait, that doesn't add up! That's too many hours and I haven't even had time for exercise, entertainment, socializing, or self-care!

My own experience is that balance for effective ministry is a matter of seasons in our life. There are some seasons when family must occupy more of the time—supervising homework, changing diapers and carpooling to the next activity—and seasons when academia takes precedence—research this paper, finish this thesis, and graduate before my family and life fall apart. There have been seasons when direct ministry, deploying to faraway places to care for the sick and injured, was the most important thing for me to do. Now a season when it has become more important to teach, mentor, write, counsel, and listen to those who are entering the season of "too much to do." Erik Erikson defined this time in my life as generativity—a time to establish and guide the next generation.

It's important to know what season of life you are in and give yourself space to wander around in it. Each season has priorities and there's no such thing as perfect balance. We will teeter and twirl, and just about the time we think we have mastered the balance, the season will change and we will learn again. We must find timely balance for effective ministry.

We Want to Run on Plenty, Not on Empty

My husband always made certain that my gas tank was more than half full. If I hadn't filled it, he would immediately take it to the local station, twenty-four miles away, and fill the tank. He wanted to be sure I would have plenty to get me home safely, again.

Most ministers have a tendency to run on empty. We don't have enough time, enough resources, enough volunteers, enough space, enough programs, enough ideas, or enough support. We are running one of the most important races of our lives and we are running on empty. How will we be safe? How will we get home, again?

If you don't want to run on empty, you must pay attention to the fuel gauge. As soon as it starts to dip, you must fill it up again. That's the beginning of self-care—paying attention to the gauge. You must be intentional about wanting to stay safe and being able to return home, again. You must watch for the signals that say you are tired, that you are micromanaging, that you are neglecting your family, that you haven't prepared your sermon or lesson or presentation. Self-awareness is a lesson in externals—what is challenging us, motivating us, exhausting us—and in internals—what I need, what I want, what I think, and how I feel. Without self-awareness, we cannot be effective in self-care.

We Want to Bounce Back—Have Resilience

Over lunch one day, Robert Wicks, author of *Bounce: Living the Resilient Life*, asked me, "How motivated are you to meet life's challenges and still be happy?" Thinking about that question, I am certain it has to do with resilience and being able to be resilient in all circumstances of life. I decided I am highly motivated to do just that!

Resilience is the ability to bounce back by coping and adapting well in the face of adversity, threats, disasters, crises, or trauma. In the microcosm of life, it's the ability to cope and adapt to the bad diagnosis, the financial insufficiency, the divorce, or the death of a loved one. Resilience is the ability to still have a healthy life after these terrible, painful events have passed. Resilience says you were able to absorb the difficulty and are not permanently damaged by the event. Your life isn't defined by those events and you are able to keep moving through the challenges, empowered by the very things that created the resilience in you.

Like muscles that are stretched and strained, some individuals become stronger as they recover from each adversity and challenge. Some people even experience significant growth as a result of the adversity. Posttraumatic growth or stress-related growth is the positive psychological change that results from adversity, allowing the individual to function at a higher level. Posttraumatic growth is not the same as resilience. Resilience bounces back to the same place, while posttraumatic growth is exactly that—growth—a higher place of functioning.

No one wants to stay stuck in grief. No one wants to stay miserable, sad, lonely, betrayed, or exhausted. We all want to bounce back. We want to be resilient.

What We Must Do

Accept Our Own Limitations
Superman is a fictional character. You are not Superman or Superwoman. You are not faster than a speeding bullet; you are not more powerful than a locomotive; and you cannot leap tall buildings in a single bound. However, you are amazingly created in the image of God with incredible abilities, powerful motivation, and deep, abiding faith. You really are pretty amazing!

We all have personal limitations that we must accept. There are physical limitations that prevent us from doing some strenuous tasks, function in high altitudes, or work in extreme weather. These physical limitations may be a result of health, age, functional disability, or physical fitness. There are emotional limitations that enable some things to overwhelm our emotions and render us unable to cope. Fear, grief, betrayal, anger, guilt, and shame are some of the most powerful emotions with which people must deal. Even when we are "the strong one" of the group, there will be times when we don't feel strong and don't want to be strong. We just want to hunker down and have someone protect us. We need someone who will take care of us.

We have limitations based on principles, values, and beliefs. We will be challenged from time to time to consider what we are willing to do and what we are not willing to do. Where's the line you will not cross?

Your values and principles will limit what you will do. Your beliefs may limit what you will do. Principles, values, and beliefs are the foundation of your character. They are what make you the person you are. You will be limited from doing some things, simply because you chose to limit yourself on principle. You will not succumb to doing anything against your principles, values, and beliefs.

Healthy self-care requires you to make some changes. There are some things you cannot change—they are outside your control. There are some things you will not change—they are outside your ethical and moral standards. Healthy self-care requires that you just accept the fact that some things cannot and will not be changed because you are not willing to change them.

Making Appropriate Changes in Our Lives

"No one likes change," is a common American witticism. Even more accurately, "No one likes to be changed." We are comfortable within the status quo. We can relax and settle into the existing state of affairs. We know what we are dealing with in that context. But are you satisfied with your stress level? Are you satisfied with your physical and mental health? Are you satisfied with your spiritual health?

Oprah Winfrey said, "The greatest discovery of all time is that a person can change his future by merely changing his attitude."[3] We can be physically, mentally, and spiritually healthier, and we must be our own agent of change. Our attitude must change from being a victim of change to a facilitator of change.

The latter part of the twentieth century and the beginning of the twenty-first century brought about some of the biggest changes the world has ever seen. With the rise of technology, change has been constant. Only those who are willing to embrace change, adapt, and re-create will survive. Change is inevitable, and change can be rewarding.

If you want to be physically, mentally, and spiritually healthy, you must make changes. You must start with your attitude—be positive—and then see yourself as the agent of change. You must initiate the changes you want to see. You must use every opportunity and resource of our technological world to help you be willing to make the changes that give you the results you want.

Start small; make one small change that is healthier than what you used to do. It could be drinking one extra glass of water each day, parking a few spots farther from the store, taking the stairs for one floor instead of the elevator, or closing your eyes and meditating on the quiet for sixty seconds. Don't try something so big you'll never do it consistently. Start small and be consistent. Enlist someone to do it with you. A partner keeps you much more motivated to make the change. Only eat dessert on Wednesdays. Use 2% milk instead of whole milk. When we conquer small changes and see the benefits, we become motivated to continue making changes. After a while, you will find it easier and easier to incorporate all those healthy actions of self-care without feeling like you are giving-up anything. They became habits and habits are hard to break.

Use Wisdom in Making Changes

Lots of people have book-smarts and lots of people have a wide range of experiences. Not too many people apply that knowledge and experience with personal awareness in such a way that they make good decisions. Wisdom requires a combination of knowledge, experience, and awareness in the context. Merriam Webster defines wisdom as "the ability to discern inner qualities and relationships" and includes such synonyms as insight, good sense, judgement, and common sense. "Psychologists tend to agree that wisdom involves an integration of knowledge, experience, and deep understanding that incorporates tolerance for the uncertainties of life as well as its ups and downs. There's an awareness of how things play out over time, and it confers a sense of balance."[4]

If we are going to take care of our own health, we must use some wisdom in deciding how we will do that. It will require some knowledge—learning about stress, learning about stress mitigation, learning about self-care, and learning about what our bodies and mind need to reach the level of good health we want.

Taking care of our own health will also require remembering our past and how we have reacted to our various experiences. We must learn from those experiences and make them meaningful in making decisions about how we will take care of ourselves from this point forward. What helped when you were exhausted and couldn't sleep? What helped when you were confused and couldn't focus? What helped when you were angry and couldn't calm down? Remembering our past experiences and letting them inform our present situation will be an important part of making decisions for our self-care.

Personal awareness within the context means even when you know a lot and have lots of experience to inform you, you must translate all of that into the context you are living within. Reflection, compassion, and truth will help guide you towards an understanding that will provide discernment and discretion and even restraint. A simple example might be that taking a short jog each day is a healthy part of your self-care. But if you have a broken leg, your knowledge, your experience, and your awareness tell you that in this context, a short jog will not be a healthy part of your self-care. Wisdom requires a balance of knowing what is good and doing what you can in the moment. Truth and reality must be a part of making those decisions, too.

Making changes to improve your self-care is a good idea. Wisdom is knowing there are some things you cannot change to improve your self-care, and there are some things you could choose to improve your self-care. Reinhold Niebuhr put it well: "God, give us grace to accept with serenity the things that cannot be changed, courage to change the things that should be changed, and the wisdom to distinguish the one from the other."[5] My prayer is that you will choose wisely.

What You Must Do if You Want More

Most people do self-care so they can be resilient, be able to bounce back after the disasters and crises of life. I think that's a good start because many people can't do that well. For others, I believe you should want more. I wasn't content with resilient. I wanted total fitness in responding to the wear and tear of my constant responses to disasters and crises of every kind on every continent. I didn't want to bounce back *after* the event was over; I wanted to be fit *during* the event. I wanted to be able to be rested even when I didn't get enough sleep. I wanted to be calm even when things were in chaos around me. I wanted to make good decisions when my mind was overwhelmed. And I wanted to be a compassionate, grace-filled chaplain even when it seemed impossible. Resilience was not enough for me.

I learned to practice some intentional habits of the heart to sustain me, to fuel me, and to keep me emotionally and spiritually healthy. These habits are the core of my self-care. When you learn what internal and external factors influence your resiliency and you actually do them as a habit, you will be building fitness, not just resilience. Optimism and hopefulness are two of the most powerful internal factors you have. Self-regulation and self-reliance will help you feel confident as you deal with the crisis, making decisions about how you will react. Flexibility and patience will keep you from breaking down and quitting.

External factors that will help you stay fit include having a strong social support network and plenty of personal resources. We need the love of others to comfort us, and we need a sense of plenty to keep giving and giving. Having accurate information and open communication will help you feel like you have some control to make decisions. Stakeholders who have a mission and believe in that mission always do better than those who have no commitment or calling to the task.

And finally, personality factors could help increase resilience and pave a way to fitness, too. Patience and creativity are key to letting you think outside the box and see things from a new perspective. And without a sense of humor and the ability to laugh at yourself, you'll have a hard time getting to fitness. You'll stumble and fall and wish you had done something differently. These are the times to laugh until you cry. Hysterical laughter is actually good for your health. It relaxes your whole body, relieving tension and anxiety. Your immune system gets boosted, and you're less likely to get sick. Laughter is good medicine.

Don't settle for good self-care. Go for more! Go for abundance. Go for fitness!

To Learn More

MacDonald, Gordon. *A Resilient Life*. Nashville: Nelson, 2004.

Paget, Naomi K. and Janet R. McCormack. *The Work of the Chaplain*. (Valley Forge, PA: Judson Press, 2006).

Swenson, Richard A. *Margin: Restoring Emotional, Physical, Financial, and Time Reserves to Overloaded Lives*. Colorado Springs: NavPress, 1992.

Wicks, Robert J. *Bounce: Living the Resilient Life*. New York: Oxford University Press, 2010.

Notes

1. Cathy Cassata, "Why You Don't Need a Lot of Time or Money to Make Self-Care a Priority," Healthline (website), September 3, 2019, https://www.healthline.com/health-news/self-care-is-not-just-treating-yourself.

2. Richard A. Swenson, *Margin: Restoring Emotional, Physical, Financial, and Time Reserves to Overloaded Lives* (Colorado Springs: NavPress,1992), 14.

3. Katherine Hurst, "Learn From The Best! Inspiring Words From Oprah Winfrey," TheLawofAttraction.com, Greater Minds, https://www.thelawofattraction.com/learn-from-the-best-5-life-changing-lessons-from-oprah-winfrey/.

4. "What is Wisdom?" Psychology Today, https://www.psychologytoday.com/us/basics/wisdom.

5. Elisabeth Sifton, ed., *Reinhold Niebuhr: Major Works on Religion and Politics* (New York: The Library of America, 2015), 705.

6

Be the Least Anxious Person in the (Virtual) Room

Margaret Marcuson

Anxiety is part of the human condition, a response to a real or imagined threat.[1] In times of great change and uncertainty, anxiety is heightened. As fast as the novel coronavirus spread, anxiety about it spread faster and to far more people. Almost a billion children worldwide experienced a sudden shift from on-site to on-line learning, and their parents had to either adapt to working from home with children present or arrange for childcare when the option of working from home was not possible.[2] Millions suffered the loss of jobs and economic stability. Businesses of all sizes struggled. Many closed. Churches and other houses of worship felt the economic impact of unemployed members even as they had to learn new ways of gathering and maintaining community online.

It's not possible to live through times like these and not be affected by the anxiety swirling around. What's a leader to do? You can't manage other people's anxiety for them, but you can work on your own. The good news is that right now you can be anxious and still be "the least anxious person in the room," as Murray Bowen used to say. Whether the room is physical or virtual, the work is the same. People are dependent on leaders to stay at least relatively calm.

Consequently, in an anxious time, leaders must attend to their own anxiety. The most important work of leaders is to manage themselves. Otherwise you can't lead, manage, or organize others. While you can't avoid catching some of the anxiety in the atmosphere, you can work to stay grounded in who you are, your purpose and your principles. You can get back on track when you find yourself reacting and ranting, even internally.

Remember that, like anxiety, calm is contagious. It may not spread as fast, but it does spread, especially in a small group like a congregation. If you are a leader, you are well positioned to influence others when you share your conviction that your community can handle this challenge. While you can't calm others down, they can "catch" your calm and calm themselves when they experience your (relatively) calm leadership.

However, it's an enormous challenge to stay in relationship with people who are anxious while still staying calm yourself. This is true whether you are watching someone's body language in an in-person meeting, scanning faces in a Zoom meeting, or listening to your mother sigh on the telephone. Anxious people want to relieve their anxiety by handing it to you, especially if you are the leader. "Pastor, I just don't know what we are going to do about Fred." "The budget doesn't look good for next year…." "We should/shouldn't do more church activities in person." Or even, "Your father is impossible!" We all have our own sensitivities to the anxiety of others, and that eye roll or sigh may cause your heart to start beating faster.

In addition, the barrage of messages from the media makes it an even bigger challenge to stay calm. The flood of news headlines, designed to promote clicks by getting your attention and raising your anxiety, is amplified by social media commentary. And of course, the people you lead are seeing similar anxiety-producing news. As a result, everyone brings a heightened state of alert into their conversations and meetings. Leaders do need to be aware of what is going on in the community and the world, especially at a time of crisis. The trick is to stay aware while remaining calm enough to respond thoughtfully.

Here are three ways to keep your anxiety in check when you notice it rising and when the anxiety of others begins to swirl your way. Your goal isn't to be completely free from all anxiety; that is an unrealistic expectation. You needn't beat yourself up if you find yourself anxious. Instead, these are three ideas to keep in mind as you provide leadership in anxious times.

First, get clear. When anxiety is high, pay attention to yourself and to your own thinking and functioning. As issues arise, whether big or small, stop and reflect. Ask yourself, "What do I think?" and, "What do I want?" If people want an immediate response, say, "I'll need a few minutes/hours/days to think about it." In most cases, an instant response is not required. Stop and think. Write something down, ideally by hand. (Handwriting helps your brain work better.) As the conversation evolves, keep asking yourself, "What do I think?" and, "What do I want?"

I talked with one pastor I coach while in-person worship was shut down due to the COVID-19 pandemic. Conversations were beginning about whether and how to resume in-person gathering. "I decided to think it through and make a recommendation to the board," she said. "We had a lot of input from the denomination and other clergy. I knew they would have their own opinions, but I wanted to start with my own thoughts." She was ready to adapt based on their input, but she went into that meeting with some initial clarity of her own. This helped her be a calmer leader in the board meeting.

As you get clear and share that clarity with others, get curious about how they react. Simply notice what they do. They may blame you for whatever problem is at hand. They may have real or virtual parking lot meetings after the actual meeting to gripe about decisions that have been made. They may derail the conversation so you don't make clear and necessary decisions or so you make poor decisions. Remember, this behavior is predictable. It's what anxious people do. Instead of blaming them, cultivate compassion for them. Don't complain about them to others. Stay connected with them. It's tempting to avoid them, but that's an anxious response in itself. Instead, be pastoral. Listen. Then, when issues are discussed, keep repeating your own thoughts in a calm manner. "Here's what I think." "Here's what I want."

Second, learn more about yourself. What triggers an anxious response in you? What are your favorite responses? We all have the typical fight/flight/freeze responses. We're biological beings. Also, we were shaped in specific ways by the families we grew up in and our position in that family. Perhaps you love a good fight, are ready to mix it up, and find it hard to let something go. Or, like me, you may be conflict averse and more inclined to flee or freeze. It takes years (literally!) to recognize and learn to manage these automatic responses. But you can start today. Simply begin to notice what you do.

One frequent response of leaders when they are anxious, or when they are confronted with anxious people, is to take responsibility for more than truly belongs to them. Many pastoral leaders grew up in a responsible position in their families of origin. Perhaps you were the oldest child or were important to one parent's happiness or security for some reason. You learned early to fix things for others. Now, you may automatically fall into the pattern of saying, or thinking, "I can fix that. I'll just [fill in the blank]." Others are happy to let you take that role as long as you will do it. Over time, this reciprocal relationship wears you out and keeps others from stepping up to their real responsibilities.

Any time and money you spend on coaching, spiritual direction, or therapy—or all three—are well worth it if you learn to recognize those automatic responses. You won't always catch yourself in time, but you can get better at recovering yourself more quickly. You can learn to ask, "Is this my responsibility or not?"

You can even use your family of origin, especially elders, to help you face current challenges. Here are two examples: Chuck Harris, a Lutheran pastor, had conversations via FaceTime with his mother from her assisted living facility as the COVID-19 shutdown began. She's in her nineties, and they talked about her experiences during World War II. "Those conversations helped me calm down," he said. "I heard more about the ways she and her family coped with those challenges when she was a little girl." He felt more able to lean into the difficulties of pastoring and parenting through the pandemic. An American Baptist pastor, Kent Harrop, called his 102-year-old Aunt Evelyn to check in. She said she was doing fine, then added, "It's not my first worldwide pandemic!" He thought she was a little confused, and then he realized she meant the flu pandemic that started the year she was born. She said, "If the first one didn't get me, this one's not going to get me. I have a great-grandson I want to get to know." He reflected, "That helps me when I get whiny." When you learn more about your relatives and family patterns, you can appreciate the strengths and capabilities that helped your family survive over the generations, through tough times as well as good ones. Those strengths are in you.

Third, keep a longer perspective. Calmer leaders are able to focus on the long-term best interests of their organization and their people. Anxiety can lead us to focus on the short-term: make this decision now, respond to this anxious person and calm them down now, avoid this difficult decision now. Church leaders, in theory, have an advantage over leaders in other organizations, because we are part of a centuries-long tradition. You can look back as far as possible, as well as look ahead. Scripture is a wonderful resource here, telling the story of God's presence with people through good times and bad, through faithfulness and failure. Your own church's history is also a resource. Look back to the founding story. Remember the challenges your church has faced over the years. Invite your people to celebrate the way your church has dealt with these difficulties in the past, even if none of them personally remember them.

Here's one example: First Parish in Concord, Massachusetts, faced a devastating fire in 1900. The building was destroyed, then rebuilt—a fully paid-for, nearly exact replica—in just over a year. Director of music Beth Norton said that as the staff discussed the shutdown of the building during the coronavirus pandemic, someone said, "We've lost our building before." They knew how to survive this situation because of the fire and the resilience the congregation had shown in the face of that disaster. Despite the trauma then and now, they knew they could get through it. One of the best examples of claiming the past during the COVID-19 shutdown was the message the Queen Elizabeth of England shared with her nation.[3] She looked back to World War II and the message she and her sister had shared in 1940 with the children of Britain who had been evacuated from London. The video was less than five minutes long, but it did exactly what it needed to do.

Our struggles are not unique in facing the coronavirus pandemic and the loss of the opportunity to gather for worship. In England in the early fourteenth century there was no communion for parishioners for six years due to a fight between the king and the pope.[4] Later that same century, the Black Plague killed two hundred million and decimated churches and communities. Millions died and churches were closed during the 1919 flu pandemic.[5] These examples, while challenging and tragic, help remind us that human beings have always faced difficulties. We can be encouraged and heartened by others who have gone before and faced these challenges.

In addition to looking back, look ahead. Take the time to think about the consequences of the decisions you are making now. In times of great uncertainty, it's hard to predict what will be true in a month, three months, or three years. However, you can ask yourself: What do I know? What don't I know? What are the convictions that will help me/us make these decisions? When leaders make thoughtful decisions based on the best information they have and solidly grounded in their principles, rather than just reacting in the moment, those decisions are likely to serve them well in the future. And they'll be better able to adapt along the way.

In some cases, church boards and congregations make decisions their pastors do not agree with. You may be the least anxious person in any kind of room and watch anxious others make choices you can't control. In this case, you can state your position as calmly as possible one more time. Then you can say you understand they have made their decision and you will abide by it. Here, keeping a longer perspective can help keep you from getting too caught up in the anxiety of the moment about a decision you think is wrong. Remember there will be other decisions to be made in the future. You can do your best to tell them what you think and influence future conversations and choices.

Finally, ongoing practices can help you notice and manage your anxiety. They help you recover your calmer self when anxiety starts to take over and you can't think clearly. They can help you stay on track day to day and moment to moment. Here are some ideas of practices to try:

1. Grow your compassion for yourself and others. Expect it to be harder to think, sleep, and focus. Accept that. You don't need to get anxious about your anxiety.

2. Focus on ways to keep yourself calm(er). Consider what has worked for you in the past and how you might adapt that to your current situation. Maybe you find cooking relaxing. Many people took up bread-baking as an anxiety-reducer while stuck at home during the coronavirus pandemic. Exercise is a proven anxiety-reducer, but maybe you can't go to the gym. You can do body-weight strength exercises in your living room.

3. Create a routine for yourself. During the COVID-19 shutdown, one pastor said he had created a routine for the church by posting prayer and worship resources three times a week, but he knew he also needed a routine for himself. B. J. Fogg, author of *Tiny Habits,* offered some terrific free trainings on creating tiny habits for working at home and other current challenges.[6] I attended several, and they were excellent. I've created some new habits that I'll be carrying into the future.

4. Breathe. Literally. One technique is to breathe in for four counts, hold for four counts, and breathe out for four counts. I do this when I wake up in the night, and it helps.

5. Manage your exposure to news sources. Seth Godin, in a post called "Calm Also Has a Coefficient," suggests, "Being up-to-date on the news is a trap and a scam. Five minutes a day is all you need."[7] Use a timer.

6. Keep up some kind of prayer practice. You can use some kind of breath prayer, such as using the opening words of the 23rd psalm in this way: Breathe in, "The Lord is my shepherd." Breath out, "I shall not want." Repeat three times, or for one minute, or for as long as you want. Or choose a favorite Scripture verse to use for prayer. If you can't stand to sit still, try walking and praying. One other suggestion: See if you can mention in prayer the name of the most anxious people who are driving you crazy. (Just the name…and trust God knows what they need.)

7. Celebrate and appreciate what you can about your current situation. Most churches can celebrate finally figuring out how to stream worship. One pastor said his church had talked about streaming services for ten years, before he even arrived, and they worked it out in forty-eight hours! That's an achievement worth celebrating. Hint: You can even look for things to appreciate about the most anxious people in your life and, if you are able, express that to them.

Whatever is going on in your life and world, the practices of celebration, appreciation, and gratitude will help you stay focused on what is right.

In summary, here's what I recommend: Get clear about what you want and what you think. Learn more about yourself and your anxiety triggers. Keep a longer perspective while developing one or two practices that can help you day to day.

However, you know yourself the best. What ideas do *you* have to lower your own anxiety by a little—even by 1% or 5%? Write them down and choose one to try out. A little less anxiety goes a long way in an uncertain environment. Being less anxious is the best contribution you can make to those around you and to our anxious world.

To Learn More

Friedman, Edwin H. *A Failure of Nerve: Leadership in the Age of the Quick Fix*. New York: Church Publishing, 2017.

Smith, Kathleen. *Everything Isn't Terrible: Conquer Your Insecurities, Interrupt Your Anxiety, and Finally Calm Down*. New York: Hachette, 2019.

Steinke, Peter L. *Congregational Leadership in Anxious Times: Being Calm and Courageous No Matter What*. Lanham, MD: Rowman & Littlefield, 2006.

Notes

1. Kathleen Smith, *Everything Isn't Terrible: Conquer Your Insecurities, Interrupt Your Anxiety and Finally Calm Down* (New York: Hachette, 2019), 4.

2. "How COVID-19 is Interrupting Children's Education," *The Economist*, March 19, 2020, https://www.economist.com/international/2020/03/19/how-covid-19-is-interrupting-childrens-education.

3. "Queen Urges 'Self-Discipline and Resolve' in Coronavirus Speech," YouTube, April 5, 2020, https://www.youtube.com/watch?v=6UPacAjWaM8. I'm grateful to Dr. Katie Long for pointing me to this video.

4. D.D. Emmons, "Church History: Pope Innocent II and the Interdict," Our Sunday Visitor, July 12, 2019, https://osvnews.com/2019/07/12/church-history-pope-innocent-iii-and-the-interdict/.

5. For a visual comparison of pandemics through the ages, see: Nicholas LePan, "Visualizing the History of Pandemics," Visual Capitalist, March 14, 2020, https://www.visualcapitalist.com/history-of-pandemics-deadliest/.

6. "Expert Help with Coronavirus Challenges," Tiny Habits, https://www.tinyhabits.com/expert-help.

7. Seth Godin, "Calm Also Has a Coefficient," Seth's Blog, March 20, 2020, https://seths.blog/2020/03/calm-also-has-a-coefficient/.

7

What Is This Time Doing to You?

Greg Mamula

In December 2019, while playing basketball with my nine-year-old son and his friends, I jumped on my way to an easy layup as I had done a million times previously.

Snap. Pain. Choice words. Collapse. An emergency room visit, MRI, and surgical consult later, I learned my right knee had sustained two torn meniscuses and a torn ACL. Turns out, being a thirty-eight-year-old is not the same as being a nine-year-old when it comes to athletic activity.

I had surgery to repair the damage on January 9, 2020. Especially in those first few weeks after surgery, everything in my life required assistance. I went through moments of grateful rest, moments of exasperated frustration, and moments of intense pain. The most difficult part was being homebound. I wanted to go to work but I could not drive, so I put in a few hours each day from home. I wanted to wear jeans but my brace would not fit, so I wore shorts in the heart of Nebraska winter. I wanted to walk on my own, but my physical therapist kept me on crutches. I wanted to go to shopping, but I could barely hobble from the parking lot to the store. I wanted to go to church and preach, but friends and family encouraged me to rest and recover. I was beginning to allow these annoyances to define my experience.

Times of challenge and difficulty have a way of revealing what dwells deep inside our souls. This happens on both personal and corporate levels. When personal tragedy strikes, our physical, mental, emotional, and spiritual competencies are all put on trial. When communal calamities occur, our collective response becomes a startling mirror we must gaze upon to gauge our social and moral health as a gathered humanity. As with all such crucibles, we discover a mixed bag of fellowship and division, hope and horror, and anxieties and affirmations.

To parse out the good from the bad, the holy from the malevolent, we need help. We need help with such reflections because we are terribly tempted to pursue paths of self-righteous justification that minimizes our complicity or, possibly worse, self-abusing disparagement. Within either extreme, things like reconciliation, restoration, healing, and hope become less likely solutions. Sometimes we are just lost in a void of uncertainty and do not how to begin.

I think this is one of the roles of pastors, priests, chaplains, and spiritual directors—the people who stand in the thin places between God and creation, ushering each into the other's presence. Barbra Brown Taylor puts it like this, "Pastors are the representative person…who walks the shifting boundary between heaven and earth, representing God to humankind, representing humankind to God, and serving each in the other's name."[1] This idea is not new of course. It originates with the apostle Paul: "I have written you quite boldly on some points to remind you of them again, because of the grace God gave me to be a minister of Jesus Christ to the Gentiles. He gave me the priestly duty of proclaiming the gospel of God, so that Gentiles might become an offering acceptable to God, sanctified by the Holy Spirit" (Romans 15:15-16, NIV). These verses speak of priestly work of gospel proclamation and standing in the gap to usher in the sanctifying work of the Holy Spirit in our lives and contexts.

At the peak of my personal frustration with my slow knee recovery I met with my spiritual director, Jeff Savage, via Zoom and vented for a while. He listened and nodded his head sagely but did not immediately respond. Hearing no objections, I rambled my way further into the seemingly one-sided conversation and shifted toward the path of naive optimism. Instead of feeling sorry for myself, surely I should use this downtime for something meaningful. I could write, do a deep study on a topic, listen to all the podcasts, master a new skill, or set a record for most viewing hours of MLB Network. Savage listened, nodded some more, and finally suggested, "Maybe it is not about what you do to this time, but what this time is doing to you." I had no idea what he was talking about.

All I wanted was get back to normal. I wanted him to affirm my desire to do ministry, to be active, to do something, anything, meaningful besides be at home. Instead we talked about the gift of limitations. Limits have their purpose in creating true freedom. Savage reminded me of what his mentor Dallas Willard once said: "Hurry is the great enemy of spiritual life in our day. You must ruthlessly eliminate hurry from your life." He followed it up with some pointed questions to me: "Why are you in such a hurry to do something? What would it look like to just be for a while?" And then the crescendo I did not want to hear: "Who you are becoming is more important than what you accomplish." I was considering adding my spiritual director to the growing list of things that annoyed me.

There is an important distinction between being busy and being hurried. Busyness is a normal product of life and full schedules. However, being hurried is an inner condition of the soul. "It means to be so preoccupied with myself and my life that I am unable to be fully present with God, myself, and with other people. I am unable to occupy this present moment. Busy-ness migrates to hurry when we let it squeeze God out of our lives."[2]

Savage was right of course. My normal life patterns had come to a screeching halt. In that silence I discovered anxiety, ingratitude, and a deep desire to be affirmed for my outward busyness dwelling deep in my soul. These flaws migrated into hurry that attempted to push God out. A hurry to heal. A hurry to work. A hurry to get back. Back to what? Back to office hours, back to shopping, back to affirmation based on productivity, back to Sunday church rhythms, back to running around pretending I am in shape? If I could just get back then I could pay attention on my terms.

Thankfully, my spiritual director boldly stood in the "shifting boundary between heaven and earth" and helped me to see what I could not see—did not want to see—on my own. He accurately discerned the deeper underlying condition of hurry and suggested I take the opportunity to observe what this time was doing to me.

I religiously did my physical therapy and returned to work in late February. I was back. I did my best to be fully present, I did my work, but I could tell I was not the same. I discovered that, like Jacob, I was carrying a physical and spiritual limp. Before I could fully reflect on that reality, the coronavirus pandemic consumed the world. After only fifteen working days, I returned home for the foreseeable future.

Beginning in March 2020, nonessential business ceased throughout the United States. Social distancing, personal protection equipment (PPE), Take-Out Tuesday, Corona-puns, and live-streaming became normal ways of life. Huge numbers of people either lost work hours or had their jobs eliminated entirely. The most vulnerable among us suffered exponentially more pain and chaos. The sudden and unexpected downtime wreaked havoc on every aspect of life. The pandemic became a mirror to our communal dynamics. Just as in personal tragedy, events like this global calamity have a way of revealing what dwells deep inside our communal souls.

Frank M. Snowden, author of *Epidemics and Society: From the Black Death to the Present*, shared with *The New Yorker*, "Epidemics are a category of disease that seem to hold up the mirror to human beings as to who we really are."[3] He gave examples of how diseases reveal inequalities in society and of how people use such times to either manipulate the chaos to consolidate more power or pursue holy justice amid such inequalities. In times of chaos we can see the best and the worst of humanity.

In times of chaos, churches, pastors, leaders, and congregants do their best to live into the ways of Jesus. During the coronavirus pandemic, I have been repeatedly encouraged by their creative adaptability and persistence. They provide online or appropriately distanced services and ministries. They gather for Zoom meetings and Bible studies. They make calls and visit one another at safe distances in driveways. They apply for Payment Protection Plan loans and denominational grants. They find ways to safely serve the most vulnerable.

In times of crisis, we are always in a hurry to "get back to normal." Despite being forced to cut back on our experiences, expenses, and exposure, we collectively remain in a hurry. When chaos strikes, we hurry to adapt to sudden change. But after a while, amid the spiritual, emotional, physical, and economic strain, communities get in a hurry to get back. Back to what? Back to the office, back to school, back to profits, back to consumerism, back to sanctuaries, back to normal. Are we in such a hurry to get back that we are missing the chance to move forward into something new? Are we in so much hurry that we have pushed God out of our collective decision-making?

When communal hurry sets in, pastors, priests, chaplains, and spiritual directors must stand in the "shifting boundaries between heaven and earth" and help us examine our corporate conditions. However, we must honestly admit that the task is too big for them alone. Fortunately, as any good Baptist will remind you, we are all priests. When addressing his collection of congregations throughout Asia Minor the apostle Peter wrote, "But you are a chosen people, a royal priesthood, a holy nation, God's special possession, that you may declare the praises of him who called you out of darkness into his wonderful light" (1 Peter 2:9, NIV). The apostle Paul told his Ephesian brothers and sisters that pastors and priests are to "equip God's people to do [God's] work and build up the church, the body of Christ" (Ephesians 4:12, NLT). Together, the people of God, in Christ, through the Holy Spirit, gathered as local congregations, are called to the ministry of God as a royal priesthood. The church is to join its pastors in representing God to humanity and humanity to God.

During times of corporate crisis, the church and all its people are called to reveal the wonderful light of Christ. Part of that process should include asking, "What is this time doing to us?" When our communities are in a hurry to return to old ways, it is our priestly responsibility to proactively examine our relationships with one another and with God. Communal challenges have a way of taking root in the areas where we are spiritually weakest. They reveal the deepest aspects of our souls. We must examine those realities in honest humility if we are ever to move forward as God intends. Crisis moments allow the church the opportunity to properly diagnose the underlying spiritual condition instead of only treating symptoms.

In an article for *Christianity Today*, Wheaton College professor and author Christine Jeske observed three areas where crisis events like the coronavirus pandemic reveal spiritual weaknesses in the North American church.[4] First, as reflected in my personal experience following knee surgery, Americans have an identity problem. Our identities are tied to what we do for a living, what contributions we make, and how full we can cram our schedules. The loss of regular productivity during times of crisis makes us feel vulnerable and without value. Pastors, church leaders, and congregations that are not providing regular services, discipleship classes, or extra curriculars feel their very identities being questioned implicitly, if not explicitly. The underlying spiritual condition is an identity problem; everything else is a symptom.

Second, the economic crash that accompanied the spread of COVID-19 revealed that Americans are not so much addicted to money as much as they are addicted to the myth of progress. When institutions such as global financial markets, schools, and shopping centers are so quickly and easily brought into submission, our belief in the "narrative of time as a steady movement toward an ever-better future,"[5] which is so deeply ingrained into our worldview, is called into question. The belief that education, growing economies, and technology will forever move us forward into an always improving age is a concept born of the enlightenment that has yet to loosen its hold on our collective psyches. Things like pandemics, terrorist attacks, and natural disasters always remind us how fragile this notion really is. Churches, leaders, and pastors feel this same pressure to constantly be on the cutting edge of progress, so we develop and utilize the latest and greatest programs and impressive graphics in the hopes it will demonstrate the relevancy of the church. Worshipping the idol of progress is the spiritual condition; everything else is a symptom.

Finally, Jeske observes that we are a people who claim to crave relationships but tend to settle for experiences. Losing so many activities, sporting events, concerts, and social engagements hurt not only because we miss seeing our friends but "because our culture teaches us that these activities make us *us*. Long before the coronavirus, we were living in an epidemic of what Harvard Business School writer Patrick McGinnis dubbed FOMO: fear of missing out."[6] Much like our desire to be defined by what we do and produce, we are also consumers fueled by a desire to prove our social worth to others. Settling for shallow, easily discarded relationships and experiences instead of incarnational depth is the spiritual condition; everything else is a symptom.

During times of crisis, whether they be local or global in scale, it is always good for the local church to slow down a little to observe what this time is doing to us. We sometimes spend so many hours and dollars finding creative ways of being productive, being an event center, or proving our value that I wonder if we have taken enough time to observe what the time is doing to us. Can we step back just long enough to ponder, "What is the difference between doing church and being the church?"

Dallas Willard's words ring in my head. Times of crisis, personal or communal, do indeed force us to change and even to slow down in many ways. But do we take these opportunities to really, truly, ruthlessly eliminate hurry from our lives? We are in desperate need of pastors and churches that boldly stand in "shifting boundary between heaven and earth" and ask, "What is this time doing to you?

Genesis 25-35 provides the narrative of Jacob. A heel-grabbing trickster, cunning manipulator, and highly gifted shepherd, Jacob was a man full of flaws. After stealing Esau's birthright and blessing, Jacob heads to his uncle Laban's until his brother's anger could subside. All his hurry stops for the briefest of moments and he rests. He has a grand vision of heaven and receives his divine blessing. Upon awaking he proclaims, "Surely, the LORD is in this place, and I was not aware of it" (Genesis 28:16, NIV). After a tumultuous couple of decades at his uncle's house, Jacob wants to return home. On the night before he meets his brother, he prays, asking God to remain faithful to his promises while scheming a way to appease his brother with gifts. Later that evening he wrestles with a man until daybreak in pursuit of a blessing.

It only comes after stating his name, "I am Jacob," and thereby confessing his true nature— deceiver, trickster, manipulator. "Then the man said, 'Your name will no longer be Jacob, but Israel, because you have struggled with God and with humans and have overcome'" (Genesis 32:28, NIV). From that day forward Jacob carried a physical and a spiritual limp. As he limped toward his brother, it was ultimately Jacob's prayer and God's faithfulness that changed Esau's heart, not the spectacle of menagerie and wealth.

I think this is the spiritual space our churches, pastors, and leaders can sit in during times of crisis. When we face crisis, it creates space to wrestle. Perhaps like Jacob we will discover that God is in this place and we did not know it because we had spent all our energy doing instead of being. Perhaps we need to exert more energy wrestling with God and confessing our true natures instead of scheming ways to appease our Esaus—our relatives, our enemies, our competitors—with elaborate offerings.

Thanks be to God we do not have to do this alone. We exist, move, and have our being in the context of community. Crisis creates time to listen and engage with the Holy Trinity and those in our community. It is okay to lament, "Where are you God? You promised to be here." It is cathartic to shout, "I am Jacob." Both assertions bring healing to individuals and community and allow us to limp into whatever comes next together.

Times of crisis give us room to ask the hardest questions. Have I ruthlessly eliminated hurry from my life so that I can allow God to attend to my soul? What spiritual conditions do I hide under hurry? How am I wrestling with God during this time? What sort of spiritual limp will I carry into what is next?

What is this time doing to you?

What is this time doing to us?

Once a crisis is over—yes, it will eventually end—the physical, mental, emotional, and spiritual limps will be collectively carried into what is next…well, those will need reflection too.

To Learn More

Chotiner, Isaac. "How Pandemics Change History." *The New Yorker*, March 3, 2020, https://www.newyorker.com/news/q-and-a/how-pandemics-change-history.

Jeske, Christine. "This Pandemic Hits Americans Where We're Spiritually Weak." *Christianity Today*, May 7, 2020, https://www.christianitytoday.com/ct/2020/may-web-only/coronavirus-pandemic-hits-americans-spiritually-weak.html.

Ortberg, John. *Soul Keeping: Caring for the Most Important Part of You.* Grand Rapids, MI: Zondervan, 2014.

Taylor, Barbara Brown. *The Preaching Life*. Lanham, MD: Cowley Publications, 1993.

Notes

1. Barbara Brown Taylor, *The Preaching Life* (Lanham, MD: Cowley Publications, 1993), 32.

2. John Ortberg, *Soul Keeping: Caring for the Most Important Part of You* (Grand Rapids, MI: Zondervan, 2014), 134.

3. Isaac Chotiner, "How Pandemics Change History," *The New Yorker*, March 3, 2020, https://www.newyorker.com/news/q-and-a/how-pandemics-change-history.

4. Christine Jeske, "This Pandemic Hits Americans Where We're Spiritually Weak," *Christianity Today*, May 7, 2020, https://www.christianitytoday.com/ct/2020/may-web-only/coronavirus-pandemic-hits-americans-spiritually-weak.html.

5. Jeske.

6. Jeske.

What We Learned About Being Church

8

The Triumph of the Quotidian—What Making Bread during a Pandemic Taught Me

Michael Woolf

Given the waning cultural influence of church in the United States, my first instinct as a pastor is to strive for creative and innovative approaches to what church should be. In 2020, I had planned for conversations about racism, gun violence, and discernment, blending the ancient rhythms of the liturgical calendar with discussions with local innovators and leaders. Of course, I only got part of the way through my purportedly blockbuster calendar before the coronavirus pandemic forced us to take our church online. Even then, my first instinct was to try to do too much, to bring that same set of ambitious proposals to life digitally, but the more I thought about it, the less that seemed to make sense. What our church needed was community, and that community is often found in the most unassuming things that we do—eating, living, and telling stories.

Pretty soon after we canceled in-person services, we launched what we called a "Take What You Need" calendar that had prayer meetings, a happy hour, children's and youth hangouts, a bread-making session, and a mid-week gathering, all of which were held virtually. The thing I, like many others, found most nourishing in this time was the rhythm of baking. It helped that there was a two-year-old in my house who could help measure ingredients while also taking premature samples of dough. If not for this crisis, I would have never had the time to start and regularly feed a sourdough starter or bake tasty bread for my family. Many folks in my congregation were in the same boat, and baking crackers, sweet treats, and bread together became a way to have conversations about our home lives that we never would have had before.

We saw each other's kitchens and the art we surround ourselves with, and we shared stories about the shape our lives were taking under stay-at-home orders. We had conversations over the whirr of mixers and the thwap-thwap of dough kneading that makes bread possible. We experienced each other in intimate ways that would never have been possible in a typical church setting that sometimes forces us to be more formal and put-together than we actually are. A real community became possible through the sharing of our efforts, and though we were able to sample what came out of our ovens, it felt like we were there for the most important part—each other. In the business of the church calendar and my desire to do exciting ministry, baking never would have made my to-do list, and yet it was nourishing to everyone involved.

I found myself thoroughly nurtured by picking up a practice that has its roots in the foundation of human society as we know it. Some of the earliest pieces of art that we have from ancient Egypt show bread in forms that would be familiar to the modern observer. In one depiction from around 2500 BC, a pharaoh is depicted at a table surrounded by slices of bread. It is a wonder that on a mighty, ancient person's tomb such an artifact of everyday life may be found. Conical pieces of bread, the preferred loaf shape of ancient Egypt, were even left at graves as food for the afterlife.

In many ways, to be human is to take grain and turn it into something nourishing. In the West that has often taken the form of bread, while other parts of the world that is more commonly linked to rice and noodles. That linkage in the western imagination of bread to nourishment is what made Jesus' proclamation, "This is my body," over bread at the Last Supper intelligible two millennia later. In our communion rites, we are invited to consider how God is linked to the bread and cup, both artifacts of everyday life that transcend time and place. In something so foundational to the human imagination, something so quotidian, we are invited to experience the Holy. It is not an exaggeration to say that I found God in the making of bread from my little sourdough culture, and I also found a connection to what it means to be human, both then and now.

In the mid-week gathering that my congregation hosted, I also experienced an ageless rhythm's lasting influence on modern life. We started out with a set theme, asking everyone to come with a poem or reflection to share on the realities of COVID-19, staying at home, and loss. People brought such amazing works of poetry, some of which they collected from various sources and others they self-authored, that I felt compelled to later produce a booklet of poems, called "Pandemic Poetry," that I circulated to the congregation. Alongside each poem I paired a picture of spring that a congregant submitted to me. The result was something that I am quite proud of, but that booklet is certainly not what people found most meaningful. Community, above all else, is what people craved during a time of isolation, and words, even beautiful poetry, could only take us so far.

I quickly realized that people were not tuning into our Zoom channel for the programming, nor were they coming to hear dynamic expressions of creativity. They were coming to see each other, to share how they were making meaning in the midst of crisis. A congregant shared that her daughter had likely contracted the virus, and we committed to pray for her. Every week, she brought updates and we lifted her concerns to God in the holy shared space we created. Another congregant was furloughed from her job, and we held her anxiety and grief as we discussed how the pandemic was likely to impact the lives of those in our community. Still another shared about the difficulties of teaching online classes and students who were not tuning into her Zoom; she worried about them slipping behind because they lacked access to technology. That opened the door to our concern for many children throughout our country who will doubtlessly be affected in ways we can scarcely imagine by the experience of living through a pandemic. Many more came to express their frustrations and concerns, sharing their missed milestones—a retirement here, an ordination anniversary or graduation there. We marked them through celebration as best as we could. People came to be seen and heard in the middle of one of the most stressful and difficult moments in our shared lives.

In this place, congregants were permitted to let their guard down, admit that everything was not OK, and be affirmed by people with whom they might not have previously been close. A matrix of connection and vulnerability was allowed to form precisely because of the lack of programming and agenda. Too often, we rush to fill any silence, especially through online media. I feared that the lack of a concrete agenda would leave congregants with an unpolished product and that they might choose not to engage because of it. The opposite was true.

Our Zoom channel became a holy space because it wasn't ambitious. It was sacred because it was a space to share what being human looked like in this difficult time. We had no ability to solve the problems that arose, only to give them a name and then to lament, cry, sing, pray, and celebrate together. Pretty soon, I realized that this was my most authentic church experience as a minister.

People were vulnerable and open in ways that I had not seen in a church setting, where there can be some intense pressure to appear resilient. I began to preach my Sunday Zoom sermons based on the concerns, questions, and reflections I heard shared during our weekly meeting. It would not be an exaggeration to say they are some of the best sermons I have preached, precisely because they were linked to joys and sorrows shared in that virtual room. Rarely have I had so much clarity about what congregants needed to hear from the pulpit. More than that, I believe that God showed up in that space, gracing us with the sacred reality of community in the midst of unprecedented upheaval. Just because we could not gather in person did not mean we were not able to experience God. Indeed, we found God more at hand in our Zoom sessions than ever before. Far from being closed, we had church in an ancient and altogether modern way. We flourished in ways I could not have predicted.

That flourishing has renewed in me a sense of trust in the Divine and in each other. It is not through my efforts that church comes into being. Church is the thing that we do together in community, or it is not church at all. Likewise, we can be confident that when we embrace vulnerability and strive to practice love and compassion more fully, God is sure to show up. These convictions are inexorably linked in scripture through

Paul's mystical naming of the church as the "body of Christ." In opening our lives to one another and creating community, we are sure to find God in that place. Once, I worried that taking church online would hinder our ability to be the body of Christ, but I found that God and community are more resilient than I gave them credit for. I was surprised, and in that surprise, I was invited to experience grace anew. For if there is one thing that is the signature of the Divine throughout scripture, it is the capacity for surprise. God comes into the world in Galilee, an imperial backwater of the Roman Empire. God identifies not with the strong, but with the weak, the downtrodden, and the oppressed most of all. God surprises throughout scripture, and in our modern world those surprises keep coming, perhaps most of all during a pandemic.

So often my ministry has meant trying to innovate or do something new, but what we needed wasn't new at all. It was all simple, daily things that helped us form community and develop resilience. Through pastoral care responsibilities, coordinating shelter options for our city's most vulnerable, and difficult decisions, a true community formed around the quotidian. This crisis meant that I had to give up any pretensions of what a modern twenty-first century church should be, and it forced my staff and me to return to basics. It was not flowery language that gave solace, but ancient words from sacred texts and prayer books. It was in the humble practice of community that an authenticity, which our spiritual forebears named as the Divine, emerged.

For churches seeking to do ministry well in these unprecedented times, the quotidian has emerged triumphant. The creation of community strains under too much initiative, too much planning, too much hustle and bustle. It thrives, like a sourdough starter, when given space to digest and share. One of the things that keeps many people from baking is the waiting, the fallow space between mixing the ingredients and placing a loaf in the oven. Yeast needs time to work its alchemy on flour, water, and salt. It does not take place on our own schedules, and it can be frustrating when baking does not align with our busy schedules. A good sourdough loaf may take as long as two days to properly prove in the fridge. Leave the mixture too long and you get over-proved bread; bake a loaf too early and your loaf more resembles a rock than the airy wholesomeness you sought. What we often fail to realize is the work that goes into making church possible also includes time and space for the holy to rise into our midst.

This is not to say that churches should do nothing. Delay too much without any action and you might miss the miracle in your midst. For my community, that meant acting swiftly in response to the homelessness crisis in our city and opening our church as the emergency shelter for our municipality. Likewise, in response to reflections in our Zoom meeting about the economic crisis, we set up a rent- and food-relief fund for non-church members in our community, making small grants to help families remain stable in troubling times. You do have to put the bread in the oven at some point, trusting that the yeast has indeed leavened your loaf with a wisdom born some 10,000 to 15,000 years ago. Action, and not just patient reflection, is required in order for the miracle of bread to be completed.

In our initial response to the coronavirus pandemic, my congregation and I learned a pivotal lesson: community, like the rising of bread, takes time and effort. In the seemingly ever-present downtime of sheltering in place, something greater than the sum of its parts was allowed to rise in our time together. One never quite believes when mixing the simple ingredients of bread that a scrumptious loaf will emerge sometime later. After a hundred loaves, it still surprises me, even though I should know what to expect. The same was true of the community that my congregation developed during this crisis. It was one of the great surprises of my life, even if I should have been amply prepared to understand it through scripture and faith.

As my church moves forward, I know we have all learned lessons we would not have learned if my calendar had been allowed to proceed as planned. Most of all, we learned we cannot simply go back to how things were; the knowledge we have gained is too precious. COVID-19 has fundamentally changed for the better our community and how we do church. We learned to take it slow, to listen to our bodies, to celebrate each other's stories and the art we produce. We learned to pay attention to a magic that was just as true in the Paleolithic period as it is now. We learned to hear anew the Lord's Prayer in its wish for daily bread, its offering of ancient wisdom for modern crisis.

To Learn More

Forkish, Ken. *Flour, Salt, Water, Yeast*. Berkeley, CA: Ten Speed Press, 2012.

Smith, Christopher and John Pattison. *Slow Church*. Downers Grove, Illinois: IVP Books, 2014.

Takenaka, Masao. *God Is Rice: Asian Culture and Christian* Faith. Eugene: Oregon, Wipf and Stock, 2009.

Zeldovich, Lina. "14,000-year-old Piece of Bread Rewrites History of Baking and Farming." *NPR*. July 24, 2018. https://www.npr.org/sections/thesalt/2018/07/24/631583427/14-000-year-old-piece-of-bread-rewrites-the-history-of-baking-and-farming.

9

"I Tell You, the Stones Would Shout Out"
—Opportunity and Renewal in the Midst of Crisis

Rachel Lawrence

The coronavirus pandemic could have been devastating to mainline churches in the United States. After all, US mainline churches have been in decline for several decades. Young people have left and haven't returned. Some families have not joined a church or religious community for multiple generations. According to the Pew Research Center on Religion and Public Life, "nones," or the unaffiliated, were the fastest growing segment of the religious landscape in 2019.[1] In this environment, churches in the United States were forced to make a difficult decision during the coronavirus pandemic. Churches had to choose between keeping religious services available for those seeking consolation and safeguarding the lives of all congregants, many of whom were in high-risk groups for the disease. This confluence of factors could have meant the end of mainline churches in the United States. But rather than remain silent as buildings shuttered, churches found new ways of proclaiming the good news to the world for our time and place. "I tell you, if these were silent, the stones would shout out," said our Lord (Luke 19:40).

The church could have been silenced. We could have decided this was the last assault and given up. Yet, as the children's song says, "The church is not a building, the church is not a steeple, the church is not a resting place, the church is a people." As such, the people of God found new ways to continue being the hands and feet of Christ. COVID-19 precautions prevented us from safely visiting in person, meeting for worship together, and enjoying the fellowship we so look forward to each week. However, many of us pivoted our tradition-bound churches to the use of new technology and renewed engagement via older means of communication, such as card and letter writing. As we did so, we found signs of new and transformed life that call to mind the words of Mark Twain in 1897: "The report of my death was an exaggeration."[2]

A Tempered Optimism

While evidence of church renewal at the onset of the pandemic did exist, the economic challenges that accompanied the shutdown were an existential threat for many small churches. Many congregations had budget challenges even before feeling the effects of rising unemployment. Many had already shifted to part-time ministry and reduced services as a result of their strained economic reality. Others had been struggling to maintain legacy buildings, and the changed economy rendered that upkeep nearly impossible. While some found renewed purpose and energy during the pandemic, others faced difficult decisions about closure and selling their buildings. Naturally, our hearts are heavy for the churches who found themselves facing the end of their ministry in their beloved settings.

I encourage churches who are under economic duress, whether as a result of the coronavirus pandemic or other circumstances, to explore partnerships with compatible congregations. In many ways, the pandemic forced us to encounter difficult truths about our churches, one of which is that some congregations had lacked the energy and financial resources to sustain a viable ministry for many years. As a people of hope in the resurrection, however, we can embrace that some of these painful changes, as we adapt to the needs of our congregations and communities, may support the long-term life of the church. With a tempered optimism that recognizes the very real pain accompanying church closures and change, we can see emerging signs of purpose, mission, tenacity, and creativity in response to crises and trying times.

Renewing Purpose

Having to close buildings during the coronavirus pandemic forced many congregations to reexamine the purpose and function of cherished traditions. Pastors and church leadership committees found themselves asking, "What do people really need from Sunday services?" and "Are we really meeting those needs?" Sunday services were once a well-attended community gathering that provided rest, reflection, and opportunity for reset from the busy work week. However, one Sunday service per week might no longer fit that purpose for members of our communities who have work weeks that include any day of the week and any twenty-four hours of the day. Rest, reflection, and reset are still very much needed, but the traditioned church has inadvertently imposed restrictions on who can benefit from worship by limiting services to an in-person, Sunday morning event. The inability to meet in-person during the coronavirus pandemic forced pastors and church leadership committees to face the reality that we were no longer effectively meeting our communities' needs. By creating online services that could be accessed during the week, we made services available to a broader segment of the public, thereby better serving the purpose of worship.

While some of the purposes of worship can be met through online media, others are difficult to meet in this way. In addition to providing a weekly period of time in which to rest, reflect, and reset, worship services have frequently served as a touchpoint for many people to connect with others socially. A key purpose churches have served is nurturing community spiritual development, and those events in our church calendar that remained active during the pandemic tended to be activities with those aims. When unable to gather physically, we used online meeting software to offer Bible studies and book groups, keep essential church meetings running, and connect through virtual coffee hours. That sense of community may not have been the same as it was before the coronavirus pandemic, but it did not become a casualty of the fight against the illness, either. Further, we were able to reach people beyond our immediate physical community. College students and people who had moved out of the area of their favorite church were able to reconnect through online platforms. This prompted churches to reconsider where the boundaries of ministries really lay as we found increasingly effective ways to minister online.

Many clergy, unable to visit those who were sick and shut-in in our communities, felt that isolation emphasized the importance of this aspect of the job. But we were able to reach out to those in isolation through other means—card ministries, phone calls, and old-fashioned letter-writing. One church near me has a significant number of members without internet or email access. The pastor adapted by mailing a letter with a sermon manuscript each week. The distance imposed by the pandemic accentuated to us that our purpose as pastors is to be with our people in their spiritual journeys at every stage of life. While many would have said this before the crisis, the inability to connect in person drew attention to how truly essential this part of our religious life together really is.

Refocusing Mission

The very nature of the pandemic forced us to deeply consider what it means to love your neighbor as yourself. With so many congregants at elevated risk, the best way to guard health and safety of our neighbors was to remain isolated from each other. The forced absence from each other provided the opportunity to think about alternative ways to care for each other. Similarly, the economic recession, with historic levels of unemployment created new needs and exposed the preexisting economic insecurity experienced by many Americans.

However, the logistics of "loving neighbor as self" were not always been clear or apparent during this time. Many churches tend to think of their mission in terms of financial giving. They define missions as money sent to do work on behalf of the church, rather than the direct work of the church. Without the regular weekly rhythm of collecting tithes and offerings, some churches did not have the funds available to send to missions they traditionally supported. Further, the economic strain created by reduced giving was deep enough that some churches struggled or failed to make their local payroll. The Payroll Protection Program loans sponsored by the Small Business Administration relieved that burden for some, but not all, churches. What did this economic reality mean for re-envisioning our mission?

The urgency of the pandemic forced us to focus locally, using our resources to meet immediate needs at hand. For example, a member of the church I serve set up a collection box for the local food pantry outside of our closed building as a way of continuing this act of love for neighbor. She had heard the urgent need broadcast by the food bank and undertook the initiative to help meet that need through this gesture. Similarly, our deacons voted to give the senior pastor at our church broad leeway to provide small amounts of emergency aid as the crisis continued. For a time, neighbor was interpreted in a more immediate and literal manner than it was previously. How this trend toward meeting immediate needs at hand will affect mission and ministry beyond local communities, including support for national and international mission efforts, remains to be seen.

Beyond locally-focused church missions, other religious and parachurch organizations pivoted from their usual work. For example, Clergy Image, a company that makes clergy apparel for women, shifted their operations to making masks and other personal protection equipment for medical personnel and other frontline workers. They also provided free cloth masks for clergy when health policy in the United States shifted towards mandatory mask use. Christian publishers and professional development providers quickly responded by producing materials to support churches with emerging model practices, seeking to adapt to a new normal. Larger church mission organizations strategized how to best respond to the many needs that emerged in the crisis. While the church doors were closed, our sense of mission was alive and well as local churches and denominations continued to work to meet people's needs out of a commitment to loving our neighbors as ourselves.

Tenacity in the Church

Driven by the renewal of purpose and mission that arose in response to the crisis, the church remained tenacious. The verse of the hymn, "The Church's One Foundation," is reflective of our collective response to the coronavirus pandemic:

Mid toil and tribulation,
   and tumult of her war,
she waits the consummation
   of peace for evermore;
till with the vision glorious,
   her longing eyes are blest,
and the great church victorious
   shall be the church at rest.[3]

The pandemic was the very definition of tribulation, to which the church responded with work, with toil. We persisted, continuing to live into our purpose and mission, and I remain hopeful that our actions will mean the continuation of a relevant and meaningful church—a church victorious—in the twenty-first century. Where did we see signs of tenacity throughout the pandemic?

The actions taken by clergy and laity to ensure continuity of community and service were evidence of the persistence of the church. Many pursued the use of technologies that were not part of the way they had previously envisioned their work. They stepped outside of their comfort zones, broadcasting church services on Facebook Live or YouTube, with whatever elements of worship they could offer. While some put together a worship experience with a skeleton team in sanctuaries, many broadcast from living rooms, from family pianos, from front porches, and more. As one of my colleagues stated, "I never in a million years thought I would be a televangelist…but here I am. I *had* to do this to keep things going." This adaptation did more than keep continuity; it began to shift the way we think about our church community.

Churches unable to support a streaming service themselves collaborated with those who could. In addition, churches found ways to offer Bible studies via video conference platforms, as well as asynchronous conversations in church groups via social media. The physical closure of our buildings was not the barrier it could have been. When physical meetings were not a viable option, we were tenacious and creative, finding new ways to continue in our worship and shared mission.

Creativity Abounds

Although the challenges and changes brought about by the pandemic created stress, these stressors also set the condition for creativity.[4] Clergy and laity had to consider what effective and meaningful worship looks like in an online medium. They had to think about various ways to make services interactive and engaging. When worship services were held in person, those who came were accustomed to the rhythm and patterns of the service. However, many elements of those services did not translate well to new online formats, such as the offertory prayer, doxology, and complicated interactive calls to worship. Early in the pandemic, one clergy member expressed concern that his attempts to provide online worship looked more like a "kidnapper demand video" than worship. These initial worries drove considerable creativity in the further development of online worship.

Within our limitations, many sought ways of making their digital worship and meeting options engaging. For example, my church's Christian education director pre-recorded children's moments that were then included in streamed services. We simplified interactive moments in the service, such as a one-line response to the call to worship and the responsive community prayer. Many churches assembled "virtual choirs," along with other pre-recorded music, to supplement and enhance online worship. Some incorporated lay readers through pre-recorded segments or through worship services on live online meeting platforms. New poetry and music was created and shared. These examples of creativity are signs of hope, life, and energy of the church that is to come.

The New Normal

We know that "normal," as we knew it, may never return. And we have probably needed to reset what we think of as normal for a long time now. The coronavirus pandemic forced us to reexamine our ministries, shining a light on long-standing systematic issues as well as emerging challenges. We should not allow ourselves to return to a state of ignorance about these issues, even after the emergence of a new normal.

The church demonstrated resourcefulness and creativity in continuing to serve our communities with mission and purpose. I sincerely hope we will continue with the same level of energy and creativity when we encounter less dire challenges in the future. The good news of Jesus Christ is as important as ever, and that message must continue to be proclaimed. The church has made much needed adaptations to continue sharing that message with the world. Our buildings may have been closed, but our hearts and message are perhaps more open than ever.

Notes

1. Pew Research Center, "In U.S., Decline of Christianity Continues at Rapid Pace," October 17, 2019, https://www.pewforum.org/2019/10/17/in-u-s-decline-of-christianity-continues-at-rapid-pace/.

2. Gary Scharnhorst, ed., *Mark Twain: The Complete Interviews* (Tuscaloosa, AL: University of Alabama Press, 2006), 317.

3. "The Church's One Foundation," Hymnary.org, https://hymnary.org/text/the_churchs_one_foundation.

4. Yongbo Sun, Xiaojuan Hu, and Yixin Ding. "Learning or Relaxing: How Do Challenge Stressors Stimulate Employee Creativity?," *Sustainability* 11, no. 6 (2019): 1779.

10
Pushed or Prompted?
God's Invitation to Change

Lauren Lisa Ng

I have always been timid around bodies of water. Never a strong swimmer, as a child I avoided walking near the deep end at pool parties for fear some jokester would push me in for a good laugh at my expense. Yet I do enjoy the feeling of stepping into water when guided by a gentle hand or of venturing past seafoam into beckoning waves, my feet sinking into the sand as my body begins to defy gravity.

Most of us prefer to be prompted rather than pushed. Not only can brute force be painful, it can also push us across the divide from present safety into unknown danger. A time of crisis, such as a pandemic, can feel an awful lot like we're being hurled into the deep end of the pool. The normalcy of our individual lives, as varied as it is, is upended. Communities face massive job loss, food insecurity, critical lapses in children's education, and a rise in domestic violence and race-motivated hate crimes, to name a few. And what of the church? In addition to addressing these concrete concerns, we feel as if we've been pushed into the deep waters of forced innovation and coerced creativity. Online worship services; concerns over how to hold interest and sustain attendance, engagement, and giving; pastoral care in the absence of physical proximity; questions about when and how to reopen buildings—we are in uncharted waters and it feels as if we've been pushed in against our will.

I've spent a good part of 2020 reflecting on the Midrashic story of Nahshon, a prince of the tribe of Judah, son of Amminidab, and brother-in-law of Aaron, the high priest. According to this tradition of rabbinic storytelling, Nahshon was among the Israelites led by Moses out of Egypt to the banks of the Red Sea. As the Egyptian army encroached upon them, the leaders of the tribes of Israel hesitated at the water's edge, debating who should go in first. As the story is told, Nahshon courageously stood up and began to walk into the sea. He waded into the water up to his ankles and the sea did not part. He waded up to his waist and the sea did not part. He waded up to his shoulders, up to his chin, and still the sea did not part. As he took the step that placed his nose under the water, the sea began to part. The origin of Nahshon's name is *Nahshol*, which means "stormy sea-waves." Despite the threat of the impending Egyptian army, Nahshon was not pushed into the water; he was prompted by God, in whose promise of deliverance he firmly believed.

If we trust that God's Spirit prompts us in times of crisis—if we believe we are never abandoned to the deep—then perhaps we can view change as an invitation rather than a forceful push. What if we are not being pushed into the deep end but are being prompted by the one who called Peter out upon the water with the simple word, "Come." (Matthew 14:29). In times of crisis we are especially attuned to the Creator's invitation to ask critical questions concerning the church's identity and purpose. The invitation has always been there, but in times of relative calm it can be easy to ignore. In these times, we have learned innumerable lessons and gained immeasurable insights about being the church, especially as it relates to our creativity and connectivity. Three areas in which God's Spirit has prompted us to engage in a deep-dive ideation process are architecture, authenticity, and constancy.

Architecture

In an address to the British Parliament in October 1943, Winston Churchill said, "We shape our buildings and afterwards our buildings shape us."[1] The topic of discussion was the reconstruction of the House of Commons, which had been destroyed by bombing during World War II. Now faced with an opportunity to redesign the building for greater capacity, Churchill's words warned against the temptation to expand based on the assumption that bigger is always better.

As the church, we design our gathering and worship spaces and then we begin to allow those spaces to determine our strategies for ministry and mission. If the sanctuary seats hundreds but our Sunday attendance is a fraction of that, we continue to pay to maintain a building that greatly exceeds our physical needs. If the nursery is far from the sanctuary, it presents difficulties if parents are needed to attend to their children during the worship service. If the building is accessible but the choir loft is not, those with limited mobility are not able to participate fully in the life of the church. You get the idea. When we don't intentionally revisit and creatively re-envision our spaces, they can start to determine the format, functionality, and impact we have as faith communities.

The prompting by God during the coronavirus pandemic to engage in this critical and creative work has led to an outpouring of innovative models. Churches meet weekly for online worship services, prayer meetings, and Bible studies. As a result, capacity and reach are virtually limitless[2] and worshipers are able to participate in events church-sponsored events they would not usually attend in person. Those previously unable to attend services due to physical circumstances, weekend shifts at work, or children's sports activities are now able to tune in online or view a recording at a later time, and many churches have actually reported an uptick in weekly attendance. The visual effect of an online meeting platform where every participant occupies the same sized rectangle on the screen has an equalizing quality that deemphasizes the line between pastor and layperson. As a result, those in leadership roles may feel permission to take a step back while those who typically assume passive roles may feel invited to participate in new ways. I know my heart has been full watching families serve one another the Communion elements each month, using whatever items they can find in their kitchens. One week my family used cookies and sparkling cider.

Our physical gatherings are also being re-envisioned by this holy prompting into uncharted waters. Not only are Sunday services taking place in parking lots with worshipers participating from their vehicles, but some churches have transformed their parking lots and buildings into COVID-19 testing sites, food banks, or temporary housing for those in desperate need of shelter. Not by pushing but by prompting, the church has been invited by the Spirit in this season to rapidly prototype a variety of architectural innovations. I believe many will remain relevant and effective long after this current crisis has abated.

Authenticity

In times of crisis we also find ourselves being prompted into the waters of authenticity. In his book, *A Hidden Wholeness*, Parker J. Palmer writes, "Afraid that our inner light will be extinguished or our inner darkness exposed, we hide our true identities from each other. In the process, we become separated from our own souls. We end up living divided lives…"[3] In other words, there is often a disconnect between how we present ourselves to the world and who we give ourselves permission to be when it seems the world isn't watching. Palmer believes this incongruity between our outer and inner selves is harmful to our souls and to the collective soul of our communities.

The functioning of the church during the coronavirus pandemic pulled back the veil on our sequestered inner selves. We are attending worship from our kitchens and living rooms, allowing others to see us in our most intimate, private spaces. We—or at least, I—show up in pajamas or sweats more often than perhaps I should admit. Kids make funny faces at the camera. The family dog lumbers across the screen. Someone's eating cereal. I believe this lack of pretense does the soul of the church some good. The time and energy we no longer commit every Sunday attending to our external selves—choosing outfits, putting on makeup, and making sure our families have chosen appropriate outfits—can now be redirected to the more important work of our internal selfhoods.

The Spirit also bids us to the waters of authentic dialogue. In a distributed church model, we find ourselves stripped of parking lot small talk and coffee hour pleasantries. Critical conversations can no longer be isolated to pre- and-post worship hallway huddles, leaving people with the feeling that these topics have been addressed by the church, even if nothing has actually been said from the pulpit. What happens when likeminded church members caucus on the topic of undocumented refugees, but the church leadership is never willing to address the issue directly? How is the church as a whole affected when BIPOC[4] church members gather after the service to discuss #BlackLivesMatter and the state of being black and brown in America, but the pastor is unwilling to formally name the church's complicity in the sin of racism? In this new way of being church, there are fewer trimmings to hide behind. While there's nothing wrong with casual talk, and fellowship is downright biblical, it cannot be at the expense of authentic dialogue and the church's commitment to prophetic voice. In this time of crisis, we have learned that being an authentic church, in a world that justifiably demands it, requires us to engage the most critical issues of our day through bold preaching, teaching, dialogue, and gospel-driven action. In the distributed church model, we have defined timeframes and vehicles by which to discern and speak the will of God. If we decide we are being pushed into the water, then we might say those parameters are limiting. But if we decide we are being prompted, we might say they are aiding the church to become its most authentic self.

Constancy

I once mastered the fairly difficult bass guitar line for a song of a band I admire. I even played it live at a show once. During this time of sheltering in place, I decided to relearn it. It took me a couple of hours to regain my muscle memory. By the end of my practice session, I was able to play it without error. The next day, I played it again with ease. Then life got busy and I went a week without picking up my bass. Sure enough, one week later, I went to play the song and I might as well have been starting again from the beginning. Almost all my memory of the bass line had been lost.

We worship the unchanging God by remaining constant in our faith. We are called to "rejoice always, pray without ceasing" and "give thanks in all circumstances" (1 Thessalonians 5:16-18); to "provoke one another to love and good deeds, not neglecting to meet together, as is the habit of some, but encouraging one another" (Hebrews 10:24-25); and to "run with perseverance the race that is set before us" (Hebrews 12:1). We are invited to continually live and dwell in God's timeless presence so that our identity and purpose will not easily fade from memory. One of the gifts we have to this end is the ability to rehearse these truths with one another. In this current crisis, we have been prompted to do so more often and in a variety of creative ways.

Prior to the COVID-19 pandemic, my teenage daughter was accustomed to attending church on Sunday morning and youth group on Wednesday night. She was well connected with a good group of friends and her faith was developing. Once we were sheltered in place, however, her youth leaders began to connect with the kids much more frequently. My daughter now engages with our church's youth ministry thirteen times a week. They offer a daily, online devotional at nine o'clock every weekday morning, a four o'clock small group every weekday afternoon, a Wednesday night youth group gathering, Sunday morning worship with the whole church, and then a Sunday evening livestream event that's just for goofing off and playing silly games. In addition, her youth leader has come by the house for a socially-distanced visit and has connected with my daughter countless times via text and social media.

The sea of change into which we have been prompted is brimming with opportunities to dwell with God in streaming format. We may be more physically isolated, but as a result we are engaging with one another on a near constant basis. This increase in weekly touchpoints impacts our human relationships as well as our journeys of discipleship as we seek to remain in persistent relationship with God. Furthermore, the smallest of gestures that mere months ago may have felt inconsequential are now the very acts that bring immense delight and hope. We are reclaiming the joy to be found in a simple phone call to see how someone is doing or a delivery of groceries to someone who cannot safely leave their home. We are even recalling that we need not make a financial transaction to show someone we care for them. A caravan car parade, a selfie video taken on our phones, a gathering of friends on Zoom, or an inspirational object left for a stranger to find (such as the painted rocks we've been seeing around our neighborhood) are all ways to sustain connection with our community and remind someone that they matter. We are rehearsing the discipline of constancy in faith, and as it bears fruit, our muscle memory is returning.

Being the First Ones In

Nahshon stood at the edge of the Red Sea and decided he wasn't being pushed into the water but was being prompted by the God of deliverance. His courageous step into a literal sea of change was in response to an invitation rather than a push. It was proactive, not reactive. In times of crisis, the church is greeted with opportunities to pursue proactivity versus reactivity as we ask critical questions about innovation, creativity, and our identity in an aberrant time. God extends to us a divine hand, invites us to come out onto the waters, and we no longer feel as if everything is breaking down, but rather, that the Spirit is breaking in.

The question becomes: How do we continually ask these questions when there is no clear crisis to remind us of the permission God gives us to ideate within the spaces of architecture, authenticity, constancy, and a myriad of other areas? If we trusted the Spirit's invitation to wade into uncharted waters more, what might we feel the freedom to try, test, or experiment with? Perhaps we fear the potential outcomes. After all, who among us can say they fully and wholly embrace change? What we do know is that the Lord our God declares, "Do not fear, for I have redeemed you; I have summoned you by name; you are mine. When you pass through the waters, I will be with you; and when you pass through the rivers, they will not sweep over you" (Isaiah 43:1-2). God doesn't coerce us to the waters of creative connectivity; God summons us. Like Nahshon, may we be the first ones in.

To Learn More

Palmer, Parker J. *A Hidden Wholeness: The Journey Toward an Undivided Life*. San Francisco, CA: Jossey-Bass, 2004.

Notes

1. "Churchill and the Commons Chamber," *UK Parliament*, https://www.parliament.uk/about/living-heritage/building/palace/architecture/palacestructure/churchill/.

2. The "digital divide"—referring to the ever-growing gap between those who have access to technology (hardware, software internet) and those who do not—is a justice issue of economic, racial, social, cultural, and political significance that must be continually addressed by the Christian church. It is important to note that not all churches have been able to transition to online offerings.

3. Parker J. Palmer, *A Hidden Wholeness* (San Francisco, CA: Jossey-Bass, 2004), 4.

4. Acronym for Black, Indigenous, and people of color.

11
Nurturing Faith at Home
Cassandra Carkuff Williams

To address the question of how best to nurture Christian faith anywhere, we must first be clear on what Christian faith is, and what it is not. Christian faith is not a set of beliefs. It is not a moral code. It is not even a lifestyle. At its core, Christian faith is a way of being that is made possible by and is utterly dependent on the grace of God made manifest in Jesus of Nazareth. While Christian faith leads to a unique way of living and of relating to oneself, to others, to other creatures, and to creation, it begins not with a set of guidelines and personal will, but instead grows from within through relationship with Jesus and the transformative experience of grace: "Instead be humble and accept the message *that is planted in you* to save you" (James 1:21b, CEV emphasis added).

The fundamental questions of faith formation are, therefore: "Can we teach a way of being? And if so, how?" Not surprisingly, I think the answer is "Yes, we can teach a way of being." However, we cannot rely primarily on the schooling methods common in church Christian education programs. Even in the church, such an approach has proven to be less effective than we might suppose. For example, while a large percentage of baby boomers and the children of boomers participated in traditional church educational programming during the 1950s, 1960s and 1970s, a small percentage of those are practicing Christians today.[1] Dedicated followers of Jesus rarely speak of the formative impact of memory verses, Bible crafts, or Sunday school curricula. Instead most speak of relationships and experiences within the faith community that drew them into discipleship. Conversely, those who chose against the faith, either deliberately or through default, consistently identify negative experiences, hypocrisy, and irrelevance as reasons for not embracing Christian faith. Effective Christian formation, whether in the church or the home, rests principally on encounter with Jesus and the experience of grace. We must, therefore, follow the model of the earliest Christian communities by taking seriously authentic Christian community itself as the primary vehicle for nurturing Christian identity.

Family is a community. In fact, family is the most formative community in the life of a child. It follows then, that family is the most powerful force for forming—or impeding—the development of Christian faith.

> Family is everything to a child. Family is the first place a child forms and experiences relationships. It is a child's first experience of community. Family is where she develops her first view and understanding of the world. . . . With that in mind I don't think it's an exaggeration to say that family is the most important arena for a child's spiritual development and soul care.[3]

As we turn to questions of faith formation within the home, we must turn our attention to what makes communities called "family" authentically Christian. Fortunately, we have guidance from the first century faith communions whose localized Jesus movement became a worldwide phenomenon. As diverse as they were, the primitive Christian communities shared a common character through which they communicated, clearly and with integrity, the presence of Jesus in their internal life and through their relationships with the larger society. This unique character manifested certain qualities and was supported by spiritual practices that are replicable in family life. Three of the qualities that consistently characterized first century Christian communities are responsiveness, grace and love.

Responsiveness

Responsiveness to changing external contexts and internal circumstances was essential to the survival of the very first Christian churches. According to Marianne Sawicki, these communities reveal, somewhat ironically, that the ability to change is one of the most conventional aspects of our

Christian heritage: "The most traditional thing about the [early] Christian churches is their adaptability, their readiness to change to accommodate new needs in new times, while preserving—more or less faithfully to be sure!—their continuity with the message and work of Jesus Christ."[3]

Sadly, when people talk about being raised in "religious" homes, they often speak of rigidity and rules. Yet, to be authentically Christian, a family needs to be a place where all members are considered learners as well as teachers, and where adults open themselves to the formative power of children's perspectives in their own ongoing spiritual formation. Early on, Christianity was known as "The Way (*hodou*) of Jesus" and its followers as "people of The Way." (see Acts 9:2; 19:9, 23; 22:4; 24:14, 22). The Greek *hodou*, translated variously as path, route, road or way, presents Christian faith as a journey of growth and change for both individuals and faith communities.[4] Responsiveness to fluctuating circumstances, changing contexts, and personal development is essential to a family life that is authentically Christian. Also essential is responsiveness to Jesus as the ultimate authority and the model for use of authority in the household.

Grace

The radical view of children that is present in the ministry of Jesus and throughout the New Testament testifies to the right of children to be raised in respectful, nurturing environments. The far too common practice of framing children's obedience to adults as obedience to God is blasphemous. Even the later New Testament writings of Colossians and Ephesians, which evidence rising institutionalization of the church and a palliative approach to the Empire, challenge the prevailing culture's emphasis on obedience. In contrast to the Graeco-Roman codes of behavior in which fathers were considered "gods" of their households, Colossians and Ephesians honor children as fully human by speaking directly to them (see Colossians 3:18-41 and Ephesians 5:22-6:9). They issue a call to shared submission to God and to compassion, kindness, lowliness, meekness, patience, forbearance, forgiveness, and love in all relationships. These writings present a perspective in which parents stand, not over and above children, but alongside them under the Lord.[5] Our faith, therefore, calls for households characterized by grace with love being the benchmark for Christian family life.

Love

Love, in Christian understanding, flows from God: "Beloved, let us love one another, because love is from God; everyone who loves is born of God and knows God" (1 John 4:7). The explication of love found in 1 Corinthians 13:4-7, so popular at weddings is egregiously absent in Christian parenting manuals. It describes love as rejoicing in the truth, being patient, being kind, and not insisting on one's own way. Parental love is an artful business. At its truest, parental love honors children as independent agents with full personhood while at the same time caring for them as "little ones" who are dependent on adults for survival, security and safety. To be a Christian community, home life needs to include acceptance of children as children. It also needs to have parameters that create safe spaces within which children can explore what it means to be alive, are free to make mistakes without fear of retribution, and are encouraged to move toward independent adulthood. Such safe spaces are maintained by a balance of freedom and structure, flexibility and guidelines, generosity and caution that adjusts as children grow.

Practices evident in the primitive Christian communities that engender the qualities of responsiveness, grace, and love include celebration, service, and trust.

Celebration

Celebration frames the life of Christian communities with one main one focus: gratitude. Practicing gratitude reminds us of the goodness of life as a gift from a loving God. As noted above, structure and routine are essential for providing children—and ourselves—with a sense of security, especially during chaotic times. Intentionally setting aside daily time for family rituals, including recreation and fun, is an existential reminder that life, while filled with challenges, is also filled with good things. Closing the day talking about what you are thankful for, reminding children that they are gifts from God, and allowing, but not pressuring, children to name or simply think about what made them happy, will end the day on celebratory note. Mealtimes are traditional moments to give thanks, however, long, wordy prayers led by adults are neither effective nor kind. More words do not make better prayers: "And when you pray, do not keep on babbling like pagans, for they think they will be heard because of their many words" (Matthew 6:7, NIV). A simple song, a recited poem, or even a brief circle dance around the table are child-friendly and child-inclusive ways of "saying grace." It is important to honor ways that children naturally express themselves beyond words, like drawing, movement, or even hugs. During times of difficulty, a family ritual of remembering past fun times and dreaming together of good times to come remind all involved that current circumstances are not determinative.

Like church rituals, family rituals celebrate God's love especially as it was—and is—revealed in Jesus. Rituals are given meaning through the stories that are attached to them, such as when we rehearse the story of Jesus' meal with his follower as we celebrate the Lord's Supper. While the Bible is a compilation of documents written by and for adults, the foundations of those documents are primarily oral and narrative. Our sacred texts hearken back to a time when extended families gathered around campfires and retold the comforting tales that formed their identity. Stories are most powerful when allowed to stand on their own without explanation, interpretation, or moralizing. They engage the imagination, which Irish poet John O'Donohue reminds us is the path of the spirit.[6] As we pass on age-appropriate retellings of stories of our faith, we need to beware that "helping" children by offering interpretations or drawing out moral lessons diminishes the story's power. To do so is also to waste the opportunity provided by the disposition of young minds.

Children think narratively. They have a greater capacity than adults to enter a story, experience it, and internalize it. A hallmark of childhood is imaginative play. Allowing children to play with stories of faith by providing sound effects or portraying the characters encourages emotional connections and discovery of what a story means for their own lives. Questions can inadvertently dictate meaning for children and rob them of agency in their faith development. Rather than ask questions with "right" answers, ponder stories together with "I wonder" statements, such as, "I wonder what the adults thought when a little boy helped Jesus feed the crowd" or "I wonder why Jesus ate dinner with people his friends didn't like." Such an approach honors children as theological thinkers in their own right and thereby encourages a sense ownership of the faith.

Service

The unique love practiced by Christians (see John 13:35). is not intended to remain within the confines of the faith community. Service beyond the Christian fellowships, including beyond family, is a type of performance art in which the stories of faith come alive as we enact and embody God's love for the world. A popular quote from Fred Rogers says that he found comfort during frightening times by practicing his mother's advice to look for the helpers.[7] Seeing people making a difference certainly offers assurance to children, as it does to all of us. Even more so, though, the power to make a difference ourselves is foundational to the joy of living life in Christ. Providing age-appropriate opportunities to help others both strengthens the critical sense of personal agency in children and honors their capacity to participate in their own faith development. When children participate in putting their faith in action, they become practicing Christians, apprentices in the life of faith. Additionally, as noted above, faith formation rests in part on encounters with Jesus. The final judgment described in the Gospel of Matthew implies that one way we encounter Jesus is through service to others. Beyond being a mandate to address the needs of those around us, Matthew 25 proclaims that Jesus identifies with the disenfranchised: "Whenever you did it for any of my people, no matter how unimportant they seemed, you did it for me" (Matthew 25:40, CEV). The gracious irony here is that as we seek to bring Jesus to those on the periphery of society, we find him already there, waiting for us. Children have natural compassion. Many of us lose that sense of concern for others not because we are fundamentally selfish, but often because that sense is dismissed by adults or because we become discouraged by the world's ability to render our efforts ineffective as we age. One of the privileges of Christian life is permission to embrace compassion and act on it. Children learn well by doing, by participating in relevant life experiences. Joining adults in service to others is a necessary vehicle for children to express their innate sense of compassion, to practice Christian discipleship, and to encounter Jesus in others.

I'd like to pause here for a moment and acknowledge it might seem that faith formation in the home would be much easier if we could just do lessons, memorize Bible verses, and instill obedience to rules. The nature of Christianity as a transformed way of being precludes any external imposition of the faith through cognition and behavioral rubrics. Creating families that function as authentic Christian communities may feel like a tall order. After all, we are only human. Yet "only human" is what God made us to be—human in relationship to our Creator. There is no app to download here. The task of creating a family that is an authentic Christian community indeed would be a daunting and impossible task if we were to do it on our own. But we do not, which leads us to the final practice for creating authentic Christian community: trust.

Trust

We are not on our own in this majestic endeavor of nurturing Christian faith in children. We noted above that the spirit of Jesus was present in and sustained the communal life of earliest Christian believers. That same spirit is present with us and is at work in family life.

One day recently, when I was feeling particularly stressed about the trials of life in this fallen world, I essentially collapsed into a chair on my porch, which is a rare move for the "doer" that I am. As I became aware of the surroundings with which I am blessed—the wintry hillsides hoping for spring, the frosty air, and song of winter birds—I heard, felt, imagined (however we frame such things) God saying, "Hey I've got this. It's not all up to you." The first job of parents and other primary caregivers may be to remind themselves that it is not up to them.

When Jesus sent his apostles out into the world, he advised them to travel light (Mark 6:8-9). Should these guidelines for creating families as authentic Christian communities become burdensome baggage, ignore them for now. Set them aside and focus instead on your own spiritual nurture. If grace is the most characteristic quality of authentic Christian community, then we must learn to be gracious with ourselves. Traditional spiritual practices, such as prayer, meditation, and Bible reading are tried and true ways to connect with God's presence, but even they can become burdensome, especially during difficult seasons of life. During seasons in life when many things are in flux, it is better not to impose rigid practices on ourselves, but instead to welcome brief moments focused on that which is unchanging. "The heavens declare the glory of God; the skies proclaim the work of God's hands," the palmist tells us (Psalm 19:1, NIV) The sun rises every morning. The moon guards each night. Lilies bloom, then wilt. Robins lay eggs. Snow falls. Each breath that sustains your body comes unbidden, a witness to our oneness with the Creator.

Will you make mistakes and have regrets in hindsight? Indeed, you will. That's why it's called it hindsight. Will there be times you feel overwhelmed or afraid or like giving up? Of course. Judging those feelings intensifies their power; accepting them diffuses it. The ironic beauty of grace is that if you give yourself some latitude and practice self-compassion, you will naturally become more gracious with others. And as keen little observers, the children with whom you share life will witness the power of grace to change lives. It is the overall tenor of your life together that will witness to faith for your children. Mistakes acknowledged and forgiven provide powerful lessons in forgiveness. Acceptance of feelings speak to honesty as the virtue that extinguishes pretense. Resting in God defeats perpetual apprehension about doing everything right.

Finally, remember that as much as you want your children to walk in relationship with God, God wants it even more. In fact, Jesus suggests that simply by virtue of being children, children are already members of the kingdom: "Let the little children come to me, and do not hinder them, for the kingdom of heaven belongs to such as these" (Matthew 19:14, NIV). God loves children when they sleep like little angels in their beds. God loves them when they lie about their homework. God loves them when they fight with their siblings or hide broccoli under the napkin. God loves them, as God love us all, just as we are. So, relax a bit. And let them relax. "Do not worry about tomorrow, for tomorrow will worry about itself" (Matthew 6:34, NIV).

Notes

1. "Barna Describes Religious Changes Among Busters, Boomers, and Elders Since 1991," *Faith & Christianity*, July 26, 2011, https://www.barna.com/research/barna-describes-religious-changes-among-busters-boomers-and-elders-since-1991/.

2. Ivy Beckwith, Postmodern Children's Ministry: Ministry to Children in the 21st Century (Grand Rapids: Zondervan, 2004), 101–102.

3. Marianne Sawicki, The Gospel in History: Portrait of a Teaching Church, The Origins of Christian Education (New York: Paulist Press, 1988), 39.

4. *A Greek-English Lexicon of the New Testament and Other Early Christian* Literature, trans. and adapted by William F. Arndt and F. Wilbur Gingrich (Chicago and London: The University of Chicago Press, 1979), 553.

5. Judith M. Gundry-Volf, "The Least and the Greatest," in The Child in Christian Thought, Marcia Bunge, ed. (Grand Rapids: Eerdmans, 2001), 56.

6. John O'Donohue, "Wisdom as the Path of the Spirit," YouTube, https://youtu.be/F0bg7lNeKY4.

7. "Fred Rogers: Look for the helpers." YouTube. https://www.youtube.com/watch?v=-LGHtc_D328. Excerpted from https://interviews.televisionacademy.com/interviews/fred-rogers, Archive of American Television.

SECTION FOUR

What We Learned
About Being Neighbors

12

"Can These Bones Live?" Christian Witness, Crisis, and the New Media Landscape

Angela Gorrell

Before spring 2020, it would have been difficult to convince most church leaders in the United States that technology should be used to discover and engage in new forms of community outreach and Christian witness. Of course, before spring 2020, some church leaders did practice their faith in digital spaces in imaginative ways and many were open to learning. However, as the COVID-19 crisis unfolded across the globe, church leaders who had not previously used much technology suddenly realized it had become critical to their ministry work. And so, by necessity, Christian communities began to use it. As they did, church leaders and members of Christian communities realized technology could help us to listen to, learn from, and nurture relationships with our neighbors, all of which are fundamental aspects of genuine community outreach and Christian witness.[1]

Several church leaders in my city came together to create a resource pantry for families in our local school district. The resource pantry offered food products, hygiene products, and other goods. Each week, the pantry used technology to update the list of needed goods. The organizers were able to use a sign-up form online to name exactly what families expressed need for, as well as to invite congregants from multiple churches to sign up online to bring those specific goods so that as many different essential items as possible were brought to the pantry each week. Numerous churches across the United States did similar things in order to feed and assist people in their communities.

Through efforts like developing resource pantries using websites and email, we learned we could use technology to efficiently meet concrete needs in immediate ways. In crisis, we realized we could update volunteers in real time so that community outreach endeavors could be managed and resourced well. We also recognized that community outreach does not have to be dependent on one organization and network of people. Instead, we saw the power of community outreach happening through hybrid—combining digital capabilities and physical settings—partnerships between organizations and their networks.

A friend of mine, Stephanie, works at an agency that serves at-risk populations, including people experiencing homelessness and individuals navigating cycles of poverty. She co-organized an online memorial for staff at the agency to honor and memorialize clients, other staff, and family members who died during the COVID-19 pandemic. People who attended were invited to lament, tell stories, and light candles from their respective locations, collectively remembering the deceased. Approximately fifty people joined. In crisis, we learned that technology can help lower barriers to belonging and participation. Anyone who could use technology to join the memorial service Stephanie helped to lead or my community's resource pantry. Many people for the first time realized Christian witness does not have to be practiced solely in person but instead can occur across time and space, both in physical and digital settings.

Chaplains at hospitals, like Stephanie, also went to extraordinary lengths to be present to people who were hurting and to demonstrate God's love. They lived apart from their families so they could continue to help without infecting their loved ones. They put their own health at risk and came up with creative ways to attend to people in hospice, like playing special music over loudspeakers. In crisis, we learned how creative use of technology could help Christians show mercy and care to people who are suffering.

People in faith communities across the United States also used social media in the midst of crisis to participate in truth-telling and advocacy. Yet again, videos of the killing of African American men—specifically Ahmaud Arbery and George Floyd—surfaced and social media posts were used to explain how people could meaningfully respond to these atrocities by calling for arrests, protesting, and demanding change. Hashtags, tweets, and status updates informed people in communities across all fifty states, helping people to organize and collaborate. The advocacy work of numerous people in Christian communities—as well as people who do not identify as Christian—did change things. Murderers were arrested and systems were held accountable. In crisis, we realized technology could help us to organize, to grieve, to express anger, and to work for justice with our neighbors.

Each of the aforementioned examples demonstrate how members of Christian communities began to truly understand how technology could be used to meet concrete needs, to share and engage in spiritual practices, to demonstrate compassion, and to inspirationally bring people together. Chiefly, Christian communities gained perspective regarding what is possible.

On the other hand, members of Christian communities also discovered ways community outreach and Christian witness should be strengthened and reimagined. Michael Stroope helpfully clarifies that witness is not the same as persuasion, argument, or coercion. Rather, witness involves beholding and telling. "To *behold* is to witness something that changes one's existence," he writes. "Beholding is more than seeing with physical eyes; it is to be captured by a vision....To *tell* is to do more than recount events with a line of argument or in a dispassionate manner; rather, *telling* is to convey with one's words and life what has been seen and experienced."[2] To witness, to behold, and to tell, is to be guided by God's love for humanity and to engage in historic Christian practices that nurture Christian virtues. It looks like imaging the life of Jesus.

Jesus did all kinds of things to flip the script on what it meant to witness to God's unconditional, passionate, fierce love. Jesus' community outreach and thus his witness was provocative. It is easy to forget this, though. Perhaps it is more comforting to only imagine Jesus as gentle and to neglect the challenging nature of his teachings and actions. One of the most alarming moments in Jesus' ministry is when he flipped tables at the temple in an act of protest against the oppressive economic system that had been set up there. Suddenly, the Jesus we often or exclusively visualize as tender and kind became angry—so angry that he overturned furniture to make a point. Jesus wanted change.

Jesus touched people who were sick and people who were dead, abandoning longstanding rules about purity. He spoke to women whom other people, for numerous "religious" reasons, blatantly tried to ignore. Often, Jesus went out of his way to build relationships with people deemed unimportant, even to commend and to heal not just physically but in holistic ways. He asked that the little children come to him and he went toward, rather than away from, people who were living with mental illness. He was always reaching out to people others tried to push away. It seems that it was precisely his flipping of the script that drew people to him as well. His constant challenging of the status quo encouraged the rich and poor, marginalized and powerful, old and young to be curious and to seek to spend time with him. Those who sought him out witnessed the living God.

Upon reflection, it seems Christian communities need to engage in prayerful reflection as to what aspects of our scripts for witness and community outreach need to be flipped. While members of Christian communities acted bravely and compassionately during the COVID-19 crisis, and some white Christians both acknowledged the horrific nature of the deaths of Ahmaud Arbery and George Floyd and did something in response, it was also apparent during and after these crises that there is much to learn and to unlearn.

Before the crises of 2020, the "dry bones" (Ezekiel 37) of white Protestant Christianity were already appearing, as evidenced by the rise of "religious nones," "religious dones," and "the spiritual but not religious" in the United States.[3] Ezekiel was a prophet in the time of Israel's Babylonian exile. In a vision, the spirit of the LORD led Ezekiel into a valley full of bones were he walked back and forth among them. It is a graphic and gruesome scene. Ezekiel remarked that the bones were very dry. Death had erased their identity, vitality, and life. The valley of bones symbolized the effect of Israel's idolatry.

Similarly, in crisis, the consequences of the white Protestant church's idolatry of power, hierarchy, and territory, along with a narrow moral regulation that is largely concerned with other people's so-called sins rather that its own, became even more visible.[4] In crisis, the ways in which white Protestant Christianity has contributed to myriad forms of death—by its complicity and contributions to inequality, injustice, and white supremacy—were brought to the forefront of white people's attention through social media, news stories, and protests. The fact that African American men and women continue to be murdered and incarcerated at extremely high rates, as well as suffering disproportionately economically and health-wise, demonstrates that white Christians have yet to truly behold and live toward a new vision when it comes to white supremacy and white ideologies that nurture systemic racism. For too many white Christians, Jesus has become a moral stranger, not a moral exemplar.[5] It is difficult to connect white Protestant Christianity in the United States with good news for the poor, freedom for prisoners, recovery of sight for the blind, and setting the oppressed free, which were the chief aims of Jesus' ministry as laid out in Luke 4:18-19.

In Ezekiel chapter 13, Ezekiel talked about whitewashed walls. Ezekiel's point is that whitewashed walls of security, where we gloss over things and cover up things to make it look like everything is OK when it is not, causes destruction. The review of history in the first twenty-four chapters of Ezekiel leaves no room for the notion of "the good old days." Ezekiel's words contribute to uncovering rather than covering up, revealing areas of concern rather than whitewashing them. In crisis, we have recognized that we cannot whitewash death nor the ways the white Protestant church have contributed to systemic racism and white supremacy.

In crisis, we see that we must instead recognize when it is midnight. Drawing on Luke 11, Martin Luther King Jr. compared situations like that of a crisis to midnight. In Luke 11, the disciples asked Jesus to teach them how to pray. Jesus taught them the Lord's prayer and then shared a parable about a person who goes to their friend at midnight, on behalf of someone else who is hungry, and is subsequently told to leave and to stop being a bother. In *Strength to Love*, King writes, "It is midnight in the parable; it is also midnight in our world."[6] He goes on to explain, "Midnight is the confusing hour when it is difficult to be faithful."[7] Many in the white Protestant church in the United States are finding it difficult to be faithful. King's beloved mentor, Howard Thurman, sheds light on why:

> Sometimes much energy is spent in a vain attempt to protect one's self. We try to harden our fiber, to render ourselves safe from exposure. We refuse to love anyone because we cannot risk being hurt. We withdraw from participation in the struggles of our fellows because we must not get caught in the communal agony of those around us. We take no stand where faithful issues are at stake because we dare not run the risk of exposure to attack. But all this, at long last, is of no avail. The attack from without is missed and we escape only to find that the life we have protected has slowly and quietly sickened deep within because it was cut off from the nourishment of the Great Exposure.[8]

In crisis, we have learned about the need for white Protestant Christians to surrender to "the Great Exposure" so that we might be more faithful and so, like Ezekiel's dry bones, we might truly live.

The Spirit also often flipped the script on Christian witness and guided the apostle Paul to places, to people, and into circumstances that he did not anticipate. In Acts 16, Paul and his companions believed they needed to go to Bithynia, but they were prevented by the Spirit from entering there. They traveled past it, and during the night Paul received a new vision of a man in Macedonia. Paul believed they needed to go there instead to preach the gospel. However, when they arrived in Macedonia, it was in fact a woman, Lydia, whose heart became open to Paul's message. Lydia's house eventually became a place of worship and later it was her home that Paul and Silas went to after prison for encouragement.

The vision Paul had for where he and his team should go changed. The vision for who Paul believed God wanted the team to preach to changed. And Paul did not initially imagine that his ministry companion in Macedonia would be a woman who owned a successful business. In crisis, perhaps God is inviting members of Christian communities to be open to the new visions of where we are going, what witness entails, and who our ministry partners are to be. Perhaps God is inviting us to minister in places, like digital spaces, and with people we have not yet imagined.

In crisis, the lack of careful attention that most Christian communities had given to new media emerged. New media is a term for a large category of contemporary forms of technology, which includes devices like laptops, streaming services such as Netflix, practices like blogging, social media, and websites. Few churches were prepared to use technology to lead worship services or to connect with congregants or their neighbors. Since 2008, social media platforms like Facebook have been used multiple times per day by vast numbers of Americans and yet, twelve years later, church leaders exhibited their limited knowledge of how new media work and to what effect. We learned relatively quickly how little thought, prayer, planning, and imagining had been given to digital spaces and mediated communication, in spite of the enormous impact of new media on people's lives, including their relationships and religious practices, beliefs, and desires.

The COVID-19 crisis demonstrated the need to spend time in prayerful discernment about Christian witness in a new media landscape so that church leaders and members of Christian communities might be intentional, careful, creative, and genuine. There are several aspects to such discernment. Part of Christian witness in a new media landscape is ensuring that people in our local community within and beyond the walls of our churches have access to technological resources and the internet, as well as the skills to use devices and participate online. In crisis, we have learned that members of Christian communities need to reflect together about the most effective ways to share technological resources and equip people to use technology, given that access to such resources and skills are critical to finding a job, networking, and other characteristics of survival in a new media landscape.

It is also important that Christian witness in contemporary culture involves addressing how new media design and use contributes to various forms of inequality, injustice, and hardship in people's lives.…. It is critical to recognize that new media spaces are not neutral spaces where everyone has equality of access, ability, power or representation, for instance. We must understand the ways that social media and other forms of new media reinforce racism and white supremacy. It is important to consider the funding sources of articles, websites, and platforms. Christians—as individuals, families, and larger Christian communities—can also address systemic injustice through careful reflection about the kinds of new media we use, how we use it, and why we use it. We can use new media, especially social media, in ways that demonstrate God's relief, compassion, forgiveness, and love. We can choose to use some design features of social media sites that nurture truthful ways of seeing and relating with others, and not use design features that contribute to competition and jealousy. Through prayerful attendance to the Spirit and to members of our communities, we can continue to imagine and to use technology to engage in revolutionary forms of Christian witness.

The kind of activities and dialogue I am encouraging necessitates an interested conversation in the new media landscape. Christians need to be interested in what God is doing in this landscape, interested in why new media is meaningful to people, and interested in what it means to faithfully practice Christian faith in person and online. Interested conversation requires prayer, fasting, and articulating clear aims for actions and words, so that Christians can try to have our means and our ends coincide. There is a subtle and yet critical line we must toe where we discern the best ways to witness to God's unconditional, passionate, fierce love in a new media landscape without exploiting or manipulating people or using our relationships, power, or influence simply as a means to an end. In other words, it is essential to not instrumentalize our social media interactions and relationships. Christians cannot simply go online with the intention of adding friends and followers in order to convert people. Likewise, community outreach requires consistently practicing storytelling, listening, intellectual humility, and the willingness to recognize that we will get it wrong sometimes and do not have anywhere near all of the answers. Genuine Christian witness is always mutually transformative, which is truly what it means to be "in this together."

To Learn More

Gorrell, Angela. *Always On: Practicing Faith in a New Media Landscape.* Grand Rapids, MI: Baker Academic, 2019.

King, Martin Luther, Jr. *Strength to Love.* Minneapolis: Fortress Press, 2010.

Lipka, Michael and Claire Gecewicz. "More Americans Now Say They're Spiritual but Not Religious." Pew Research Center. September 6, 2017. https://www.pewresearch.org/fact-tank/2017/09/06/more-americans-now-say-theyre-spiritual-but-not-religious/.

Lipka, Michael. "In U.S., Decline of Christianity Continues at Rapid Pace." Pew Research Center. October 17, 2019. https://www.pewforum.org/2019/10/17/in-u-s-decline-of-christianity-continues-at-rapid-pace/.

Stroope, Michael W. "Toward Pilgrim Witness." Epilogue in *Transcending Mission: The Eclipse of Modern Tradition.* Downers Grove, IL: IVP Academic, 2017.

Notes

1. Portions of this chapter adapted from Angela Gorrell, *Always On: Practicing Faith in a New Media Landscape* (Grand Rapids, MI: Baker Academic, 2019).

2. Michael W. Stroope, *Transcending Mission: The Eclipse of Modern Tradition* (Downers Grove, IL: IVP Academic, 2017), 371. Emphasis his.

3. Michael Lipka, "In U.S., Decline of Christianity Continues at Rapid Pace," Pew Research Center, October 17, 2019, https://www.pewforum.org/2019/10/17/in-u-s-decline-of-christianity-continues-at-rapid-pace/. See also Michael Lipka and Claire Gecewicz, "More Americans Now Say They're Spiritual but Not Religious," Pew Research, Center September 6, 2017, https://www.pewresearch.org/fact-tank/2017/09/06/more-americans-now-say-theyre-spiritual-but-not-religious/. "Religious dones" are people who report that they once affiliated with a religion but no longer affiliate with any religion; this is otherwise known as religious deidentification. "Religious nones" are people who report that they are not affiliated with any religion.

4. I offer this critique as a white Christian who has spent my life attending Protestant churches, most of which were majority white. I write as someone who loves the church and believes in the power of the collective church. I write in humility and with conviction, recognizing there is a lot of work to do and I want to be a part of a way forward that acknowledges sin, works against racism, invites anti-racism, and nurtures life and not death.

5. Miroslav Volf discussed Jesus being a moral stranger during a conversation at the Yale Center for Faith and Culture to me and our colleagues. However, he

did not make a direct connection between white Protestant churches and this notion in the way I am in this chapter. It was more of a general reflection on Christianity in the United States.

6. Martin Luther King Jr., *Strength to Love* (Minneapolis: Fortress Press, 2010), 53.

7. King, 61.

8. Howard Thurman, *Meditations of the Heart* (Boston: Beacon Press, 1953), 44.

13
What Are We Learning About Community?

Marilyn Turner-Triplett

> *But he wanted to justify himself, so he asked Jesus, "And who is my neighbor?"*—Luke 10:29, NIV

"There is no way to understand postwar Europe and the world without an in-depth confrontation between our ideas of mankind and the remains of Auschwitz." So reads the homepage of the Auschwitz-Birkenau Memorial and Museum.[1] Auschwitz was one of the locations I visited some twenty years ago, during a brief period of overseas study that included the nation of Poland. My study cohort was blessed with a sensitive and knowledgeable guide who encouraged us to take time to encounter the physical elements of the camp while absorbing its emotional impact.

As a result of his counsel, I felt the iron gates that announced an unholy welcome to the death camp. I could hear the clang of the rustic cattle cars rolling on train tracks designed to usher more than a million men, women, and children to an assembly line version of mass murder. I listened to the shadowy footfalls of those long-ago internees as they escorted me along the gravel pathways bordered with unforgiving barbed wire, one path leading to the gas chambers and another to the prolonged suffering of the camps. The hairs on my neck tingled when I passed under the watchtowers silently manned by the ghosts of the SS guards who, with the power of life or death at their fingers, watched the detainees' every move. My study cohort traveled from a cramped, dank, and unlit bunk house to the deadly showers. But unlike our ethereal companions, upon our exit, we retained the ability to breathe and to walk. And so we walked to the ovens, where their real or imagined stench clung mulishly to my nostrils.

Horrific experiences all, but the one that remains most vivid for me surrounds our visits to the places of the ledgers: the gas chamber center that contained the salvaged hair and teeth of those who had been slaughtered and the material evidence facility that housed the personal possessions of detainees who'd been deceived into believing they were being taken to a place where such trivialities mattered. It was the ledgers that I found most horrifying. Page after page of meticulous, excruciatingly neat, handwritten records tallying shoes, hairbrushes, toys, toothbrushes, clothing, mirrors, jewelry, and more. Thick, carefully bound ledgers that precisely detailed the dates these items had been confiscated. Sterile, accurate ledgers that bore damning witness to the unchallenged belief that a Star of David insignia or a state's declaration that some people group was "undesirable" was enough to strip away the shared humanity of millions. It was all so arrogantly callous and impersonal.

For the United States of America, the May 25, 2020, police killing of George Floyd became such a ledger. The image of a seemingly unremorseful white man pressing his knee into the neck of a Black man for eight minutes and forty-six seconds once again forced this nation to wrestle with our collective understanding of the nature of race, economics, access to resources and the meaning of community. This eight minute and forty-six second ledger— interspersed with the cries from the witnesses to "Please, stop, you're killing him" and coupled with Mr. Floyd's own pleas for his mother—calls us to an uncomfortably familiar place of reckoning, lamentation, and horror.

It calls us to a place of surrender, demanding that we release any presumption of innocence in the face of this nation's racist past. It is simply not good enough to proclaim, "I wasn't even born when all that happened." This ledger, written in the blood and tears of our ancestors, calls us to acknowledge that this nation's history has shaped our collective psyche and continues to inform our current reality and limit our future potential. It is a ledger that is calling us to a place of repentance, making it inarguably clear that the time to challenge the casual acceptance of white privilege is long past due. It is an ugly and ancient ledger carefully bound in hate, fear, lies, indifference, self-justification, greed, and economic disparity that has left many in America to ask, "Who is my neighbor?" And so, in the face of a pandemic that had already cost the souls of so many, some Americans once again decided to abandon attempts at justification—to perhaps, at long last, confront and rebuild the flawed foundation of our democracy.

I was one of many who virtually attended the televised memorial services for George Floyd. At the invitation of Al Sharpton, I stood, praying and weeping in my family room, for eight minutes and forty-six seconds in recognition of the torturous time Mr. Floyd endured prior to his death. In those long minutes, it became apparent to me that if we are to become a united nation—if we are to see one another as neighbors—we must collectively lament, repent, speak truth, and listen to one another. We must begin our journey together. We must engage in the hard, sometimes unrewarding, even punishing work of community building.

To begin our journey toward community, we must acknowledge the bitter fruit resulting from this nation's first roots: the theft of the land we all live upon from her Native People, the theft of their cultures, the sin of the ongoing internment of many on under-resourced reservations, and the intentional use of language, names, images, and phrases that remain socially acceptable despite their offensive nature. We must acknowledge this nation's construction on the bloody backs of the Black women, men, and children—a people who were stolen from their native lands; whose intellectual property was, and continues to be, demeaned in its own context while also being eagerly used to garner unearned profits for their oppressors; whose enslavement in the most brutal, destructive form of slavery in human history continues to permeate and plague every aspect of life in twenty-first century America.

We must allow those eight minutes and forty-six seconds to call to mind the racially-based abuse of persons from all Asian cultures from the time they came to these shores in search of the so-called American dream; to the period during World War II when Japanese Americans' freedom and livelihoods were stripped away as they were placed in state-sanctioned internment camps located on the soil of this nation; and to this very moment in time, when Asians and Asian Americans are targeted for abuse and discrimination by those who erroneously blame them for the coronavirus pandemic. Those achingly long eight minutes and forty-six seconds cry out for our acknowledgment that, in the case of brown Spanish-speaking people, we have denied the heart of the "Mother of Exiles" and have grown deaf to her song to "Give me your tired, your poor, Your huddled masses yearning to breathe free...."[2] We must own the realities of the brown children in cages who are still separated from parents and denied entry into this nation; the people who are labelled as undesirables, thugs, rapists, persons to be feared, and drug dealers; the people who are good enough to ensure our food chains remain intact by doing the work most Americans won't, but not good enough to escape the labeling that comes with brown skin and Spanish-speaking tongues.

Those eight minutes and forty-six seconds implore us to realize that if we are to truly become a nation of neighbors, we must call out the gender biases and the casually accepted sexual subjugation that continue to overshadow our daughters, wives, sisters, nieces, lovers, friends, aunts, and mothers. We are contaminated by the virus of disregard for womanhood; even the church has no immunity against it, as demonstrated by the refusal of some churches to acknowledge the gifts and calling of women to positions of leadership.

This ledger is a reminder that it is past time to acknowledge that our nation's churches have fallen short of a Christ-centered perspective of what it means to be community because of our refusal to grant equal access to our LGBTQ sisters and brothers. Negative perceptions regarding the LGBTQ community is one of the last bastions of church-supported discrimination. We choose to ignore the study, conducted by Chapin Hall at the University of Chicago, informing us that, while they comprise just 7% of the total youth population in the United States, LGBTQ youth comprise 40% of all youth experiencing homelessness.[3] Additionally, the study found that "LGBTQ youth are at more than double the risk of homelessness compared to their non-LGBTQ peers;"

that they "had over twice the rate of early death among youth experiencing homelessness;" and that "youth who identified as both LGBTQ and Black or multiracial had some of the highest rates of homelessness."[4]

America's ledger does not end in our past; it continues to destructively influence our current realities. In his May 17, 2020, interview on *60 Minutes*, Federal Reserve chairman Jerome Powell provided an economic basis for why community restoration is essential. Powell shared that when people are out of work for a prolonged period, their skills begin to atrophy, they lose contact with the workforce, and their careers become damaged. Powell affirmed that because of the COVID-19 pandemic, the most important indicators for national recovery are medical ones that suggest keeping workers at home. He applauded Congress for its swift action to help people pay bills and retain some sense of solvency. He recognized that the economic road to recovery for this nation could be prolonged and bumpy and that this is a time of great suffering and difficulty where unemployment could go as high as 25%. But he also stated another reality. Those who are being hurt the worst during this pandemic are, to an extraordinary extent, women, the most recently hired, and the lowest paid. Powell noted that among people who were employed one year ago and making $40,000 or less, almost 40% have lost their jobs. Our ledger shows that far too often, this group of people head the households that our nation's poorest children call home.

A study conducted in 2016 found that "among all children under eighteen years in the US, 41% are low-income children and 19%—approximately one in five—are poor."[5] There can be no doubt that this nation can and should be doing more on behalf of children. Childhood poverty is an epidemic that is consuming our nation, yet we seem content to exist in a state of denial about its virulent and destructive nature. Perhaps the complexities of poverty are sufficiently overwhelming that many choose to proceed with great caution. But these are times when an overabundance of caution is benign malevolence. Silence and inaction, in the face of these evils, is a form of violence. The quote often attributed to Dietrich Bonhoeffer says it best, "The test of the morality of a society is what it does for its children."

The scourge of childhood poverty not only impacts families and communities; it also hinders this nation's ability to compete in the future. When children thrive, we thrive; when they fail, we fail. Coming of age while living in poverty is an immense threat to robust childhood development. But, if we choose to, we can be effective in halting the march of childhood poverty. Studies have proven that early, long-term investments of time and caring in the lives of low-income children produces tangible social and economic results.[6] Economist and Nobel prizewinner James Heckman challenges our nation to improve the economic prosperity of the United States by striving for improved living conditions and better life outcomes for our children.[7] If Jesus' caution against forbidding children access to the abundance of life[8] is not enough to serve as a call to action on behalf of our children, then perhaps the awareness that it makes economic sense to do so will suffice.[9]

While public health officials advise social distancing to decrease the spread of the novel coronavirus, many low-income jobs cannot be performed remotely, and the cramped housing and crowded neighborhoods where many of our nation's poor live prohibit any notion of social distancing. None of this is news to us. According to the Joint Economic Committee's 2020 report, "The Impact of Coronavirus on the Working Poor and People of Color," there is an expectation that the poor, the working poor, and people of color will suffer disproportionally from any recession resulting from the pandemic. Because of the overrepresentation of Blacks and Latinos in the service sector, they are hardest hit by massive layoffs and stay-at-home orders. Native American populations suffer from similar challenges, many of which are exacerbated by limited community access to the resources necessary for combating a major viral outbreak. Overcrowding and a lack of access to clean water, which is necessary for handwashing to prevent the spread of the virus, are also issues that disproportionately affect Native American communities.[10]

One result of persistent discrimination is that these people groups generally have less accumulated wealth to help them survive any economic crisis. On June 1, 2020, the nonpartisan Congressional Budget Office reported that the US economy won't fully recover from the coronavirus pandemic until 2029—a nine-year recovery that, assuming there will be no need for a second closing of the country, won't begin until 2021. What will this mean to America's poor, especially poor people of color who tend to experience poverty at higher rates than whites? What will become of our nation's children?

We may finally be learning that a community-oriented nation will choose to grapple with these questions as if our lives depend on finding virtuous solutions. Because they do. We may finally be ready to acknowledge the truth of the relational words of Martin Luther King Jr.: "Whatever affects one directly, affects all indirectly…I can never be what I ought to be until you are what you ought to be. This is the interrelated structure of reality."[11] We may be preparing to consider and embrace the philosophy espoused by Kenyan-born John Mbiti: "I am because we are, and because we are, therefore I am."[12]

As a direct result of the largely youth lead movement surging across our nation, we are beginning to see glimpses that national well-being is grounded in relationship. A multicultural collective of young people, many too young to vote, are coming together to insist that we address and overcome racial and socioeconomic injustices in these United States. And across the country people of every age, political affiliation and social standing are responding. There is evidence of the beginnings of change.

In 2016, the National Football League (NFL) condemned Colin Kaepernick for taking a knee during the national anthem in protest of police brutality and racial inequality in the United States. Donald Trump weaponized Kaepernick's protest to ignite further polarization of the nation by calling his actions unpatriotic. But in early June 2020, NFL commissioner Roger Goodell issued an apology. He tweeted: "We, the NFL, condemn racism and the systematic oppression of Black People. We, the NFL, admit we were wrong for not listening to NFL players earlier and encourage all to speak out and peacefully protest. We, the NFL, believe Black Lives Matter. #InspireChange."[13] It remains to be seen how that apology will evolve.

In its June 1, 2020, statement regarding the movement sweeping our nation, NASCAR acknowledged a need to do more in a statement that read, in part, "While our sport has made progress over the years, there remains much work to be done and we fully embrace our responsibility to help bridge the racial divide that continues to exist in our country. We must do better and our commitment to promoting equality and inclusion continues and will never waver."[14]

For the first time since its 2013 launch in response to the acquittal of Trayvon Martin's vigilante murderer, the message of #BlackLivesMatter is being considered by a broader spectrum of Americans. The Black Lives Matter (BLM) mission quickly resonated among many African Americans, but it was targeted for distortion by political pundits, hate groups, and unions with messages like #WhiteLivesMatter or #BlueLivesMatter. Sadly, some churches, including many in the Black church, were complacent in attempts to water down the message with counter-calls of #AllLivesMatter. Now, the aims of BLM—to eradicate white supremacy, to build local power to intervene in violence inflicted on Black communities, to combat and counter acts of violence, to create space for Black imagination and innovation, and to center Black joy—are resonating with large audiences.

We celebrate the tentative steps we are taking but would be foolish to ignore the potential pitfalls that lay ahead of us. Conservative commentators continue to choose to debate the "merits" of George Floyd as a martyr. It is an inane argument, but for those seeking to justify themselves and the preservation of the status quo it is an appealing argument, one that is based in the assumption that Blacks should not rally around a person unless that person has lived an exemplary and blameless life. I wonder how many of our s/heroes in Scripture would pass such a litmus test. Would we celebrate Rahab the prostitute, Moses the murderer, Mary Magdalene with her history of mental/emotional challenges, Paul the politically privileged mass murderer, Peter the impetuous knife wielding coward, the woman at the well with her questionable past, the Samaritan—despised because of his heritage, or Mary, the mother of

Jesus—pregnant before she was married? Would Jesus, a young man who was intentional about breaking laws and challenging the status quo, make the cut?

What will become of this movement? Americans tend to resist the hard work associated with in-depth analytical thinking and grace-filled dialogue with persons of diverse views. Instead, we embrace representative solutions that invite diverse voices to tables traditionally dominated by white male voices but avoid the hard work of incorporating the messages those diverse voices bring. We are a nation with a microwave mentality; we insist upon instant answers and instant gratification. What we face is the result of an accumulated disregard of our shared humanity; addressing it will require a slow cooker mindset. White America must own its accountability and participate in the search for meaningful solutions. Is this nation up to that? We will need to guard against those who seek to polarize the movement based on landmines such as the issue of defunding the police, a lightning rod issue that will require serious dialogue and informed listening. The movement will be at risk of division based on questions of inclusivity, messaging, leadership, generational perspectives, focus points, and more.

In the final scenes of the movie *The Help*, the African American maid, Aibileen Clark, confronts her vindictive employer, Hilly Holbrook, a white woman committed to the promotion of racism. Stepping forward to look her directly in the eyes, Aibileen declares, "All you do is scare and lie to try and get what you want. You're a godless woman. Ain't you tired, Miss Hilly? Ain't you tired?" Ultimately, America's progress will be dependent on how truly tired we are. Policies, legislative reforms, and laws will only take us so far. The ability of this latest movement to achieve true community is dependent on the condition of our hearts. But, as the prophet Jeremiah reminds us, "The heart is devious above all else; it is perverse—who can understand it?" (Jeremiah 17:9). So, like Aibileen I ask: Ain't you tired, America? Ain't you tired?

I pray for a response that demonstrates that our nation's heart is thoroughly fatigued by the burden of denial, self-justification, and sound-bite thinking. I pray for the fierce spirit of tenacity that calls on wisdom, creative genius, intellect, courage, and love to engage in the difficult work of community building. Only then will we be blessed with a nation that lives up to our ideals.

To Learn More
Kendi, Ibram X. *How to Be an Antiracist.* New York: One World, 2019.
Wilkerson, Isabel. *The Warmth of Other Suns.* New York: Vintage, 2011.
Rothstein, Richard. *The Color of Law: A Forgotten History of How Our Government Segregated America.* New York: Liveright, 2018.
Bouie, Jamelle and Rebecca Onion. *The History of American Slavery.* Produced by *Slate.* Podcast. May 18, 2015–October 13, 2015. https://slate.com/podcasts/history-of-american-slavery.

Notes
1. "Education," Auschwitz-Birkenau Memorial and Museum, http://auschwitz.org/en/.
2. Emma Lazarus' famous sonnet depicts the Statue of Liberty as the "Mother of Exiles," a symbol of immigration and opportunity; symbols associated with the statue to this day. Source: National Park Service, Statue of Liberty, https://www.nps.gov/stli/learn/historyculture/emma-lazarus.htm.
3. "Our Issue," True Colors United, https://truecolorsfund.org/our-issue/.
4. M.H. Morton, et al., "Missed Opportunities: LGBTQ Youth Homelessness in America" (Chicago: Chapin Hall at the University of Chicago, 2018), 3, https://voicesofyouthcount.org/wp-content/uploads/2018/05/VoYC-LGBTQ-Brief-Chapin-Hall-2018.pdf.
5. Heather Koball and Yang Jiang, "Basic Facts about Low-Income Children: Children Under Eighteen Years, 2016," (New York: National Center for Children in Poverty, Columbia University Mailman School of Public Health, 2018), 1, http://www.nccp.org/wp-content/uploads/2018/01/text_1194.pdf.
6. Eric Westervelt, "How Investing in Preschool Beats the Stock Market, Hands Down," *NPR,* December 12, 2016, http://www.npr.org/sections/ed/2016/12/12/504867570/how-investing-in-preschool-beats-the-stock-market-hands-down.
7. James Heckman, "Key Quotes," *Center for the Economics of Human Development.* University of Chicago. https://cehd.uchicago.edu/wp-content/uploads/2016/12/Quotes_2016-08-02_mb.pdf.
8. See Matthew 19:14, Mark 10:14, or Luke 18:16.
9. Marilyn Tuner-Triplett, *Justice for Rizpah's Children: Radical Responses to Childhood Poverty* (Valley Forge, Pa: Judson Press, 2018), 2.

10. Maria Givens, "The Coronavirus is Exacerbating Vulnerabilities Native Communities Already Face," *Vox*, March 25, 2020, https://www.vox.com/2020/3/25/21192669/coronavirus-native-americans-indians.

11. Martin Luther King, Jr., "Remaining Awake Through a Great Revolution," *Commencement Address for Oberlin College*, June 1965, Oberlin, PA, https://www2.oberlin.edu/external/EOG/BlackHistoryMonth/MLK/CommAddress.html.

12. Undercover Reporter, "John S. Mbiti: 'I Am Because We Are, and Because We Are, Therefore I Am," Undercover Africa, October 8, 2019, http://undercoverafrica.com/john-s-mbiti-i-am-because-we-are-and-because-we-are-therefore-i-am/.

13. "Goodell says NFL was wrong for not listening to players," *AP News*, June 5, 2020, https://apnews.com/cb4639c897d7fc6445ca4ceb9514b66d.

14. "NASCAR Statement on Current Civil Unrest," NASCAR.com, June 1, 2020, https://www.nascar.com/news-media/2020/06/01/nascar-statement-current-civil-unrest/.

14

Responding to the Rising Tide of Mental Illness

Greg Johnson

In December 2004, the world witnessed a catastrophic event unlike any seen before as various news outlets broadcast the aftermath of the deadliest tsunami in history. The destructive wall of water destroyed towns and cities along the coast of the Indian Ocean. Nothing in its path survived. Pictures and video of the affected areas showed empty places where homes and buildings previously stood. According to the World Health Organization (WHO), "as many as 280,000 people lost their lives and more than one million people were displaced."[1] The trauma extended well beyond the moment in which the catastrophic events occurred. Over ten years after the tsunami, in 2016, an earthquake struck the Indonesian island of Sumatra. Fearing another tsunami, many Sumatrans were reported "crying and screaming as their memories of the 2004 tsunami were triggered."[2]

Large-scale disasters change not only the social fabric of a society, but they also result in emotional and psychological effects that resonate long after the initial event. While attention is given to the physical well-being of those impacted, the psychological trauma has the potential to last far longer than physical maladies. The WHO noted, "Survivors are likely to spend years wrestling with the mental health impact of the Asian tsunami and the earthquake off the Indonesian coast."[3] "Severe mental health problems, such as psychosis or severe depression, typically affect 2–3% of any given population but can increase to 3–4% after a disaster," the WHO said.[4] The tsunami that upended the coasts of Indonesia and neighboring countries drastically altered the lives of those affected. While mental health services were required immediately after the 2004 tsunami, mental health experts indicate that mental illness could increase 10% after a catastrophe.[5] As workers from the WHO provided counseling for the population, it was noted that the mental health burden in Sri Lanka was higher than 50%.[6]

Studies have shown how people continued to be impacted by the September 11th terrorist attack on the United States.[7] First responders and individuals living in close proximity to the event were found to suffer significantly with post-traumatic stress disorder (PTSD). "The disorder involves substantial functional impairment and is often comorbid with other mental health conditions such as depression, generalized anxiety disorder, or substance abuse. For these reasons, PTSD is the most commonly studied disorder in the aftermath of disasters."[8]

As with these catastrophic events, lives were dramatically and drastically altered by the coronavirus pandemic. Hundreds of thousands died from COVID-19, leaving loved ones to grieve. Millions more were diagnosed with the disease or confirmed as asymptomatic carriers of the virus. Health care systems struggled to meet demand. News reports brought daily updates of the number of deaths, infections, and survivors. Economies stalled under the weight of shelter-in-place orders and restrictions on business activities deemed non-essential. Unemployment skyrocketed. The emotional and psychological effects of this global crisis will continue to be felt long after it subsides.

In the United States, *The Washington Post* cited polling by the Kaiser Family Foundation indicating that nearly half of adults reported the crisis impacted their mental health and 19% said it had a "major impact."[9] The challenge of addressing these concerns will be influenced by the demographics, economics, education, gender, and age of those affected.

The pandemic spotlighted racial and ethnic disparities in access to behavioral health care including barriers to mental-health and substance-use treatment services.[10] Within African American communities, these barriers include a general mistrust of healthcare providers that is rooted in past experiences of neglect and abuse, and stigma concerning mental health conditions and their treatments. For many, mental illness is not normalized but is seen as a fault within the individual.

Then there is the severe strain on frontline workers in the healthcare field. Nurses, physicians, and other hospital personnel working long hours in crisis situations face their own personal mental health challenges. Many experienced burnout and depression as well as the stress of possibly contracting the virus. "The pandemic is likely to have both long and short-term implications for mental health and substance use. Those with a mental illness and substance use disorders pre-pandemic, and those newly affected, will likely require mental health and substance use services."[11]

In this crisis environment, many might not have access to therapeutic care due to social distancing protocols. While social distancing is necessary, it limits access to support groups upon which individuals with mental health concerns depend. James Lake and Mason Turner, both medical doctors, argue that "mental illness is the pandemic of the 21st century" and the next major global health challenge.[12] Lake and Turner note that one-third of the adult population deal with some aspect of mental illness. In 2009, the *American Journal of Public Health* reported that in 1999 "about one in four Americans had a mental health disorder and two-thirds of those mental disorders did not receive treatment."[13] In 2019, statistics from the WHO revealed that one in five individuals experiencing conflict or crisis "is estimated to have depression, anxiety, post-traumatic stress disorder, bipolar or schizophrenia."[14] Logically, these statistics most likely will increase in the aftermath of the coronavirus crisis.

Eventually the coronavirus pandemic will wane and in its wake will be survivors who are traumatized emotionally, mentally, and spiritually. As the tide of mental illness rises, many dealing with mental health conditions will be a part of communities of faith, as some are now. As previously mentioned, people turn to their faith in challenging times. Studies suggest that 90% of Americans have turned to their own religious tradition to manage trauma. Even those who did not have a faith tradition also found religion to be helpful.[15] Individuals with mental health conditions also found comfort in religious beliefs. Researchers concluded that religion serves as a "pervasive and potentially effective method of coping for persons with mental illness."[16] Unfortunately, churches in the

United States have not traditionally been places of support for mental illness. Nonetheless, there is a growing need for communities of faith to provide space for healing as individuals deal with unresolved grief. Anxiety and depression are inherent in the aftermath of a crisis. Some individuals will possess the resilience to pick up the pieces of their lives and continue moving forward, while others will struggle with losses that took a toll on their lives. During the early stages of shelter-in-place orders, sanctuaries were empty. Moving forward, plans for regathering should include providing support for individuals living with mental illness. When these efforts are embraced by faith community leadership, they have a higher level of success.

A mental health ministry can be strengthened when churches connect with community-based mental health providers and organizations to assist individuals and make referrals when needed. Mental illness should not be the leprosy of the twenty-first century. Pastors and clergy should reach out to social service agencies to collaborate on efforts such as community-based partnerships. National organizations can also provide resources and guidance with developing a mental health ministry including Pathways to Promise, NAMI FaithNet, and the American Psychiatric Association's Mental Health and Faith Community Partnership.

It is essential that clergy and lay leaders learn to identify the signs of mental health challenges like anxiety and depression. Members of faith communities initially may not feel comfortable disclosing their mental illness. However, when the community of faith normalizes mental illness—that is, embraces it as a normal part of life—the door is opened for individuals to feel comfortable disclosing their mental illness.

Becoming familiar with mental health conditions can be helpful to clergy and lay leaders because these conditions impact an individual's spiritual growth. This doesn't mean leaders need to be diagnosticians concerning mental illness. Those educated would be able simply to recognize congregants that exhibit signs of depression, especially when they suddenly withdraw from participation in community life in the absence of significant, life-changing events.

When clergy are sensitive to their congregants' mental health, it indicates that they are concerned about the well-being of the individual. Here is where ministry to "the least of these" can be most impactful. However, oversimplifying mental illness by spiritualizing it is not helpful. Mental illness will require more than the application of prayer and scripture. While prayer and scripture may provide comfort, those with mental health conditions need the same level of medical attention as would those living with diabetes, hypertension, or cancer.

Incorporating a health ministry that provides mental health resources would be a monumental step towards being sensitive to this population of people. Inviting mental health workers along with social service workers and agencies to collaborate with such a ministry provides support to the church. These agencies and organizations can provide training and facilitate ongoing conversations about mental illness which would further normalize mental illness.

Other ministries beyond the church may help provide additional support including chaplaincy or spiritual care. While chaplains are spiritual companions that walk with individuals on their spiritual journey, they possess a unique skill: that of the ministry of presence. The ministry of presence is non-judgmental and non-anxious. Those who practice the ministry of presence do so with the deepest of respect for the individual and their journey. Communities of faith that do not practice the ministry of presence border on being segregated when they are called to be open to anyone who desires to be affiliated. After being socially isolated, the ministry of presence will be inviting to those who may be looking for a community of faith that is welcoming. As with the aftermath of September 11th when scores of individuals sought sanctuary in churches as they dealt with their emotional trauma, many may look to the church for refuge in the aftermath of this and future crises.

The ministry of presence allows individuals with mental health conditions to feel safe and welcomed. Here is where the church can meet the needs of individuals living with mental illness by providing a safe, non-judgmental, and non-anxious space that nurtures community. In this non-judgmental and non-anxious space, grace abounds. Grace is acceptance without bias. Those who extend the ministry of presence avail themselves to receive grace in this nurturing relationship as well. Grace nurtures relationships, and it brings persons who are open and vulnerable together. This is where the gospel of Jesus Christ comes to life.

With online and virtual worship, new and emerging ways of being the church have begun to take shape. Communities of faith may want to reshape life together by establishing small group ministries that are spaces for grace and sharing mental health concerns. How communities of faith deal with the rising tide of mental illness has the potential to shape new paths for ministry or alienate a population that desperately needs to belong. As a new profile of ministry emerges, there is the possibility of hope for those living with mental illness.

Now is an excellent time for faith communities to embrace mental health as a vital aspect of ministry. Mental health ministries will fill a significant void that exists, and partnering with community and social service agencies will enhance the quality of ministry for those living with mental health conditions and their families. Continuing to neglect a population of people who need to feel welcome in the body of Christ helps neither those individuals nor the body of Christ.

For too long, mental health needs and concerns have gone unnoticed or overlooked in church life. Every church, no matter the size, has the potential to reach out to individuals with mental health conditions and their families. In doing so, the heart of the church will prove sufficient to minister with those with mental health conditions—those who need not live in the shadows of our life together.

To Learn More

Pruyser, Paul W. *The Minister as Diagnostician: Personal Problems in Pastoral Perspective*. Philadelphia, PA: The Westminster Press, 1976.

Williams, Lavern, Robyn Gorman, and Sidney Hankerson. "Implementing a Mental Health Ministry Committee in Faith-Based Organizations: The Promoting Emotional Wellness and Spirituality Program." *Social Work Health Care* 53, no. 4 (April 2014): 414–434. https://www.ncbi.nlm.nih.gov/pmc/articles/PMC4000587/.

Notes

1. Haroon Ashraf, "Tsunami Wreaks Mental Health Havoc," World Health Organization, June 1, 2005, https://www.who.int/bulletin/volumes/83/6/infocus0605/en/.

2. "Post Earthquake and Tsunami Mental Health Care in Aceh," JSI.com, April 6, 2017, https://www.jsi.com/post-earthquake-and-tsunami-mental-health-care-in-aceh/.

3. Ashraf, "Tsunami Wreaks Mental Health Havoc."

4. Ashraf.

5. Ashraf.

6. Ashraf.

7. Yuval Neria, Laura DiGrande, and Ben G. Adams, "Posttraumatic Stress Disorder Following the September 11, 2001, Terrorist Attacks: A Review of the Literature Among Highly Exposed Populations," *American Psychology* 66, no. 6 (September 2011): 429–446, https://www.ncbi.nlm.nih.gov/pmc/articles/PMC3386850/.

8. Neria, DiGrande, and Adams, "Posttraumatic Stress Disorder."

9. Joel Achenbach, "Coronavirus is Harming the Mental Health of Tens of Millions of People in U.S., New Poll Finds," *The Washington Post,* April 2, 2020, https://www.washingtonpost.com/health/coronavirus-is-harming-the-mental-health-of-tens-of-millions-of-people-in-us-new-poll-finds/2020/04/02/565e6744-74ee-11ea-85cb-8670579b863d_story.html.

10. "Double Jeopardy: COVID-19 and Behavioral Health Disparities for Black and Latino Communities in the U.S.," *Substance Abuse and Mental Health Services Administration,* April 15, 2020, https://www.samhsa.gov/sites/default/files/covid19-behavioral-health-disparities-black-latino-communities.pdf.

11. Nirmita Panchal, et al., April 2020), "The Implications of COVID-19 for Mental Health and Substance Use," Kaiser Family Foundation (KFF), August 21, 2020, https://www.kff.org/health-reform/issue-brief/the-implications-of-covid-19-for-mental-health-and-substance-use/.

12. James Lake and Mason Spain Turner, "Urgent Need for Improved Mental Health Care and a More Collaborative Model of Care," *The Permanente Journal* 21 (2017): 17–42, https://www.ncbi.nlm.nih.gov/pmc/articles/PMC5593510/.

13. Marc A. Safran, et al., "Mental Health Disparities," *American Journal of Public Health* 99, no. 11 (November 2009): 1962–1966, https://www.ncbi.nlm.nih.gov/pmc/articles/PMC2759796/.

14. "Mental Health in Emergencies," World Health Organization, June 11, 2019, https://www.who.int/news-room/fact-sheets/detail/mental-health-in-emergencies.

15. Harold G. Koenig, "Research on Religion, Spirituality, and Mental Health: A Review," *The Canadian Journal of Psychiatry* 54, no. 5, (2009); 283.

16. Koenig, 285.

SECTION FIVE

What We Learned About Our Nation

15
Our National Homework Assignment—
Beginning to Envision a Just and Inclusive Society
Jeffrey Haggray

America was brought to a standstill by the coronavirus pandemic, with authorities telling us, "Stay Home!" The rapid spread of COVID-19 stalled the engines of our society. Systems of transportation, industry, education, business, entertainment, sports, and hospitality and even religious gatherings came to a screeching halt while operations in healthcare, crisis management, public safety, and government were stretched beyond their capacity to serve all those exposed to the deadly coronavirus.

Moving forward, we would do well to reflect critically on the plight of countless vulnerable people whose dire circumstances were exposed by this pandemic. During this crisis our nation and world have been overwhelmed with the painful realities of sickness and death. However, we must acknowledge that unwarranted suffering and death in America did not start with this pandemic. Countless vulnerable and voiceless Americans, many of them among the working poor, have been struggling to survive our political and economic systems for years, and their plight has been seldom discussed in the halls of government, in houses of worship, in corporate America, or in our entertainment-driven culture.

Hindsight is 20/20. How Did We Arrive at This Point of Vulnerability?
At the start of 2020, many people suggested it would be the year for seeing everything clearly. Little did we know that 2020 would bring so many painful realities in our nation into such sharp focus. What has the pandemic revealed about the health of our nation and how did we get here? Overcoming our present predicament and repositioning ourselves for a new normal require that we understand how we arrived at this

point of vulnerability. Then, through a form of "humanitarian contact tracing" we can locate our affected and suffering neighbors and begin to get needed aid to them, while also strengthening our core to resist against future suffering.

For many years now, public theologians, justice advocates, community-based organizers, health and human service advocates, educators, and many others have repeatedly sounded the alarm in the public square for increased compassion and justice, demanding a cessation to business as usual and begging government officials at the national, state, and local levels to pursue equity in the distribution of resources for the greater good. Through public witness and advocacy work with the American Baptist Home Mission Societies and service on the boards of various non-governmental organizations, I have joined efforts calling attention to the suffering of vulnerable people, while watching basic protections diminish day by day.

The list of ills undermining the quality of life for countless Americans is far too long to itemize here, but no humanitarian reset is possible unless we name the maladies, which include: persons wasting away in America's prisons and jails at a huge cost to our basic humanity and budgets; migrants detained in cages along our southern borders; uninsured persons lacking access to lifesaving healthcare; persons with mental and physical disabilities and addictions dying on our city streets; victims of human trafficking suffering from forced labor and sexual imprisonment; persons striving daily against food scarcity; impoverished public schools lacking the basic resources and supplies needed to provide quality education to our nation's children; digital deserts where underserved populations lack access to vital technology and internet service; elderly and sick persons barely surviving in isolation without the community support that makes for a healthy life; and extreme poverty across our nation that relegates countless people to a wretched existence of despair, addiction, hopelessness, and often homelessness. This is merely a partial list of the long-term suffering experienced by millions of persons in the wealthiest nation on earth.

All these vulnerabilities have been exposed at various times in America prior to the COVID-19 pandemic, whether by large-scale natural disasters such as Hurricanes Katrina and Maria, or during mass social protests in underserved communities in the aftermath of police brutality, or by numerous documentaries and campaigns calling attention to the plight of America's poor. Moreover, conditions among all the above populations have worsened dramatically under the Trump administration in recent years. We would be derelict of ethical responsibility were we to ignore that reality. America's rich have grown richer[1] while conditions affecting the poor have worsened.[2] Speaking on MSNBC, Eddie Glaude of Princeton University pointed out that the national emergency prompted by the COVID-19 pandemic "exposes the fault lines in America" caused by extreme capitalism.[3]

The White House and the Congress took emergency measures to slow the spread of the disease and to shore up the healthcare industry by injecting money into the economy in order to prevent a complete financial meltdown. Nevertheless, for many years now we have witnessed a systematic unraveling of America's safety net for its most vulnerable citizens on the part of all branches of government—executive, legislative, and judicial—and at all levels including federal, state, and local.

The government has unwisely sacrificed billions in needed tax revenues to increase the profits of the wealthiest Americans and to satiate unharnessed capitalist greed, while the safety net for millions of other Americans has been torn asunder. As America's social and economic infrastructure has diminished and protections for everyday people have waned, the federal government has spent trillions of dollars on wars, weaponry, and military activities under the banner of national and homeland security, which is of no consolation to us now as hospitals, doctors, and healthcare workers are sacrificing their lives without adequate equipment or protections on the frontlines of the deadliest public health crisis in one hundred years. Who knew that the greatest threat to our nation in generations would be the coronavirus pandemic?

20/20 Vision for a Just Future

Now is the time to attend to our long overdue national homework assignment. I encourage everyone, from church leaders to government officials, from business leaders to non-profit leaders, and from all industries, whether corporate, travel, hospitality, entertainment, sports, private, public, or religious, to consider the following question: What would a public policy reset look like across America—at the federal, state, and local levels—with regard to caring for the most vulnerable people in our land, whether they are citizens or undocumented residents? Reset is defined here as starting over from the beginning to envision a just and inclusive society. Given the many painful realities that are now exposed concerning the poor state of our internal health as a nation, how might we envision, implement, and sustain a nationwide safety net that assures everyone has access to a living wage, safe food, clean water, housing, healthcare, education, protection from unjust incrimination, and freedom from injustice, abuse, and degradation?

Visioning a Healthier Nation Through the Lens of Easter

In the weeks leading up to Easter Sunday 2020, President Donald Trump instigated a public debate about whether to attend church on Easter Sunday.[4] Trump was not genuinely concerned about the faithful attending their houses of worship during the Resurrection observances. His priorities related to the economy were well established in the public record. Instead, Trump wanted to see the "stay at home" restrictions caused by the pandemic lifted across America in order to restart the economy. Having claimed that the stock market, the economy, and the employment numbers reflected his successful leadership as president, he feared that the flatlining of those categories signaled his failure. I joined faith leaders across the nation urging Christians to resist Trump's foolish temptation to gather in churches at the height of the pandemic.

Among the impediments to addressing the needs of poor, underserved, and endangered populations across our nation has been unrestrained support for Trump's leadership from the most loyal segment of his political base, namely white evangelical Christians, as they characterize themselves. I will simply note that in the sequence of the adjectives just given, the word white appears first and Christian appears last. Therein lies the challenge with compelling Trump and the politicians controlling the U.S. Senate and the courts to provide the resources needed to improve conditions for underinsured, underemployed, and underserved Americans. So long as white privilege in America is prioritized above Christian compassion for the least of these, we will lack the political will to improve the quality of life for all Americans.

Followers of Jesus should use this time of crisis to cast a vision of the quality of compassion, humanitarian concern, and intervention needed to strengthen our nation's core with respect to the wellbeing of all Americans. Federal, state, and local governments must coalesce with non-governmental organizations, faith communities, and the private sector to raise fundamental questions regarding the welfare of millions of people whose extreme vulnerabilities are now exposed in the areas of public health, public safety, education, income inequality, access to food, housing, healthcare, and technology. The only way to uncover any semblance of a silver lining behind this dreadful pandemic is to exercise vigilance in searching for it.

Visioning a healthier nation through the lens of Easter requires Christians to remember that Holy Week observances mark the shameful suffering of an innocent person caused by dishonest dealings, false reporting, and injustice. Resurrection unfolds only slowly, though brilliantly, in the aftermath of unwarranted suffering and death. Our Lord's resurrection was discovered by frightened and vulnerable followers when an angel of the Lord asked them, "Why do you look for the living among the dead? He is not here, but has risen" (Luke 24:5). Said another way, why do you seek new hope amid the old normal? Christians survive in this world on the hope that life eventually overcomes death after long periods of unwarranted suffering. We must lean in hard and courageously in order to insist on new resources, new possibilities, new legislation, and new life for communities that have lost hope in a healthy future.

In the financial recovery initiatives approved by the federal government in response to the coronavirus pandemic, we saw that the only thing preventing America from uplifting the quality of life for all people is a lack of will. As discussions loomed concerning sheltering in place, working from home, providing paid leave and emergency relief, a social media post went viral concerning how America could have been providing relief to persons in distress all along.[5] The writer stated, "Children could've gotten laptops and free Wi-Fi this whole time....Abandoned federal buildings could've been used for homeless people....Bill payments could've been furloughed this whole time....Evictions could've been delayed this whole time....Humanity could've been humane this whole time."

The Convergence of Two Viruses – COVID-19 and Racism-20

Sadly, in the spring of 2020, America witnessed an outbreak of a second deadly virus on top of the coronavirus: racism. Just as we were envisioning a way forward to a new normal, our nation was hit once again by a viral outbreak of violence against Black and brown bodies at the hands—and knee—of white police officers and vigilantes. Americans are rediscovering the harmful risks associated with carrying on business as usual while refusing to confront the underpinnings of racial, social, and economic injustice.

Within the span of one month, the deaths of three Black citizens—Ahmaud Arbery, Breonna Taylor, and George Floyd—captured and seared the consciences of Americans of all races, cultures, and persuasions. The murders of Ahmaud Arbery by white vigilantes in Brunswick, Georgia, and of George Floyd by four police officers in Minneapolis were captured on video. Both revealed the savage and vile hatred of racist perpetrators indiscriminately robbing and destroying the lives of vulnerable Black males with a vicious hastiness that makes COVID-19 appear slow and hesitant. All the victims similarly deprived of their lives have died because of a prevailing virus in the body politic of America that takes for granted that Black lives do not matter and that Black people have no rights that white people are guaranteed to respect.

Within twenty-four hours of seeing the cellphone video of George Floyd gasping, "I can't breathe," and dying on a Minneapolis street beneath the weight of Officer Derek Chauvin's knee on his neck, our nation moved from debating how to reopen cities without a vaccination or testing for the coronavirus to highly charged mass protests involving tens of thousands of Americans on the city streets demanding justice for those slain by racism and by police violence. Consider some of the parallels between the coronavirus pandemic and racism in America: Both viruses attacked a segment of our population that can least withstand an external assault from such a deadly enemy. Racism, like COVID-19, is indiscriminate in its attacks on Black and brown bodies, not caring whether they are emergency medical technicians, college students, security guards, or executives, nor caring whether they are jogging or birdwatching. Racism's widespread devastation, like COVID-19, is also rooted in a long history of intentional neglect followed by denials of responsibility for our nation's long and sustained history of abuse of people of color.

What can faith communities do to reduce the devastating effects of COVID-19 and of racism on vulnerable communities? While specific responses will vary from one community context to another based on demographics, passions, and the strengths of the respective congregations, there are some actions that all Christians can take regardless of their social and demographic context. What follows is a highly generalized outline for social action on the part of the faithful.

Engage in Public Witness and Advocacy

Public witness and advocacy involves efforts conducted largely in the public square, including:

1) *Giving ethical and moral critique publicly* to shed light on the socioeconomic, ideological, and political policies that create and sustain the inequities and injustices we see in our communities, whether in public health, policing, public education, housing, local economy, employment, etc.;

2) *Voter education and mobilization efforts* is raising awareness in the pews, in neighborhoods, and among policymakers at the local, state,

and national levels to influence public policies that advance shared community values. Voter registration, education, and mobilization activities are intended to elect policymakers who covenant to remain accountable to the concerns of all community members.

Form Intentional Communities

Modeled on the Beloved community depicted in Acts 2:44-47, intentional communities will model the values of our faith informed by unconditional love, the doctrine of *imago dei*, and unconditional justice. Such community models give attention locally to quality education, healthy lifestyles, access to health care for their members, sharing resources in economically- and environmentally-friendly ways to address community needs, and providing safety, shelter, and sanctuary (emotionally, physically, spiritually, financially) for persons who come in search of community.

Discipleship in intentional communities calls upon the faithful to live in a state of humility toward our neighbors and ongoing spiritual formation for ourselves that includes prayer, the rejection of injustice, and caring for the most vulnerable among us in the pursuit of healing (see 2 Chronicles 7:14).

Prophetic preaching in intentional communities declares that justice secures our nation, but the failure to behave justly toward the least of these undermines the security of our communities and our nation. It also declares that when we reorganize community values around the needs of the poor in spirit, those who mourn, the meek, those who hunger and thirst for justice, the merciful, the pure in heart, the peacemakers, and those who are falsely persecuted, and when we answer Christ's call to be the salt and light in the world (see Matthew 5:1-14), then God will guide us in changing our condition.

Invest Heavily in Emerging Generations

Whatever intervention strategies we pursue to combat COVID-19 and racism, we must consciously and sternly embrace a focus on younger populations who in fact are the most vulnerable in every community. From preschool to college years, from young adult workers to young families, age matters. The youngest members of our communities are still forming their personal identities, personal faith and value systems, sense of vocation, and educational, financial, and career foundation. It is time for us to invest all we can in those on the horizon. Make sure they have moral and community support, financial wherewithal, education and training, and the keys to our church buildings.

Young people cannot survive the tumults of future years simply on a lecture, a wing, and a prayer. They need to be given trust, resources, mentorship and coaching, unconditional love and the raw materials needed to engage the world as highly engaged global citizens and persons of faith. Every responsible adult should be able to identify young people, even beyond their own family tree, that they are pouring into by way of encouragement and support. This kind of investment is not to be codified only in a last will and testament. Rather, this kind of investment needs to become part of the daily service of us all.

Notes

1. Alexander Tanzi and Michael Sasso, "Richest 1% of Americans Clost to Surpassing Wealth of Middle Class," Bloombers, November 9, 2019, https://www.bloomberg.com/news/articles/2019-11-09/one-percenters-close-to-surpassing-wealth-of-u-s-middle-class.

2. Tim Henderson, "Poverty Grew in One-Third of Counties Despite Strong National Economy," Pew, December 19, 2019, https://www.pewtrusts.org/en/research-and-analysis/blogs/stateline/2019/12/19/poverty-grew-in-one-third-of-counties-despite-strong-national-economy.

3. Ali Velshi, "Dorothy Roberts: We Need a Radical Transformation of the Structures that Support Working Families," MSNBC, March 28, 2020, http://www.msnbc.com/ali-velshi/watch/dorothy-roberts-we-need-a-radical-transformation-of-the-structures-that-support-working-families-81332293630.

4. Miranda Bryant and Oliver Laughland, "US Christian Leaders Criticize Trump's Easter Coronavirus Deadline," The Guardian, March 25, 2020, https://www.theguardian.com/us-news/2020/mar/25/trump-coronavirus-easter-christian-leaders-respond.

5. Mississippi Rising Coalition, "Just a thought: COVID-19 is showing you the facts that American capitalism has lied about," Facebook, March 21, 2020, https://www.facebook.com/MississippiRise/posts/1567059853458627.

16
Will Our Union Be a Victim of Crisis?

Marvin A. McMickle

Will we still be the United States of America after the threat of COVID-19 has passed? In 2020, the notion of our being fifty states united in common cause has been severely tested. It has sounded at times as if we were governed by the 1781 Articles of Confederation, rather than by the US Constitution of 1787 that begins with the words, "We the people of the United States...."

We did not seem united when it came to stay-at-home policies to slow the spread of the novel coronavirus. Many states never issued such an order, and others started too late to prevent the virus from taking root in their communities and possibly spreading to neighboring states. We did not seem united when states were forced to bid against one another in the open market to secure ventilators, surgical masks, and Personal Protective Equipment (PPE), all because there was no federally coordinated process. This, of course, drove up the price, and it also disadvantaged those smaller states that could not maintain a bidding war with New York or California.

We did seem united when the president insulted various state governors simply because they did not agree with his timetable to reopen the country to economic activity. We did not seem united when the president told his millions of Twitter followers to "liberate" states whose governments had enacted restrictions in the interest of public health.[1] We did not seem united when protesters carrying semi-automatic weapons at Trump-inspired rallies gathered in front of various state capitols waving confederate flags and banners with the Nazi swastika.[2] When unarmed, nonviolent Black protesters took to the streets to seek changes in policing after the shooting deaths of Ahmaud Arbery, Breonna Taylor, George Floyd, and Rayshard Brooks during this same period of time, they were called terrorists and instigators. When Trump-inspired militia groups stormed into the state capitol in Michigan, they were heralded for exercising their Second Amendment right to bear arms.

We did not seem united when states began to reopen their economies on separate schedules, despite the fact that none of those states met the federal guidelines on how to reopen safely, beginning with the requirement that there be no increase in new cases over the preceding fourteen days. Predictably, states like Florida, Texas, Arizona, North Carolina, and Arkansas that were among the first to lift stay-at-home orders saw the biggest spike in new cases of COVID-19 as people returned to bars, restaurants, beaches, bowling alleys, barber shops, and beauty salons, often without wearing a mask or maintaining social distancing. In our haste to return to normal in terms of our national economy, we made matters worse in terms of ending the spread of this disease.[3]

We did not seem united when US-born Asian Americans became the victims of hate crimes, simply because the virus may have originated in China.[4] When Governor Andrew Cuomo of New York pointed out that most of the cases of COVID-19 in the Northeast were the result of people traveling into this country from Europe, and not from China, there was no anger or hate directed at them.

We did not seem united when centuries of social neglect caused African Americans and Native Americans to die from COVID-19 at a rate that greatly exceeds their percentage of the national population. There has always been some question, even in the original language of the U.S. Constitution as to whether those groups were ever meant to be part of the United States of America. Perhaps that question is now being answered. It was disheartening to discover that in my hometown of Chicago, African Americans make up about 32% of the population, but accounted for 72% of the deaths associated with COVID-19. That same pattern appears in states across the country. Jocelyn Wilder, a doctoral student at the University of Illinois School of Public Health, noted in the *Chicago Tribune* that we should "attribute the difference in mortality and infection rates to socioeconomic factors that preceded the epidemic."[5]

The tragedy brought on by the COVID-19 pandemic is not a matter of theodicy, or human suffering that is the result of God's will, directed toward humanity as punishment for our sins. This is not something God is doing to us. This is a virus whose effects are made worse by centuries of neglect by this nation towards parts of its population. As Elvia Diaz of *The Arizona Republic* put it, "That COVID-19 is disproportionately killing African Americans is horrific and deplorable. But it is only shocking to those who have turned a blind eye to the plight of communities of color in this country."[6]

We do not seem united when higher rates of high blood pressure, diabetes, obesity, asthma, and heart disease make African Americans more susceptible to being impacted by and dying from this virus. Living in poverty, not having access to affordable health care, not having access to fresh meats and vegetables, and being reliant on public transportation that makes social distancing impossible are major contributors to these higher rates of infection and death. The *Chicago Tribune* reports that "food and pharmacy deserts are concentrated on the South Side, and eight of the ten ZIP codes with the highest percentage of people without cars are on the South and West sides."[7]

We do not seem united when this nation's centuries-long history of racism has resulted in overcrowded housing, low-paying jobs, limited access to preventive health care, and an economic position that forces too many African Americans to use emergency room services as their primary source of medical care. We get sicker more easily because of these preexisting and underlying conditions referred to as comorbidities. We may die from COVID-19, but we were made more vulnerable to the effects of the virus because of so many existing health problems that allowed the disease to take hold of our bodies with more deadly results.

To gain some perspective on this present crisis, I urge everyone to consider that this is not the first time that socioeconomic factors have made African Americans especially vulnerable during a deadly outbreak of disease in this country. In his biography of Richard Allen, the founder and first Bishop of the African Methodist Episcopal Church, Richard

Newman reminds us that when yellow fever swept through Philadelphia in 1793, "Black residents were particularly vulnerable because they did not have the money or means to leave the infected area."[8] Additionally, many Black Philadelphians were put at risk when they were recruited to work on the front lines caring for the sick.[9] Then, as now, African Americans have not only been the victims of a deadly virus; they have also been among the first responders as they cared for other sick and dying people in hospitals. We have never been united when it comes to Black and brown people in this country. It seems that "We the people of the United States" was never meant to include all the people of the United States.

This brings us to another way in which we do not seem to be united in this country. Much has rightfully been said about the great work done by medical professionals and first responders, such as ambulance drivers and police officers, during this pandemic. However, we have discovered other essential workers who had not previously been fully valued in the United States. Who cleans the rooms and transports the patients in hospitals? Where would we be today without farm workers, bus and truck drivers, mail carriers, food delivery drivers, restaurant cooks, and janitorial workers inside all kinds of businesses? Their essential work has kept the nation moving during this crisis.[10] Many in this group have been asking for a living wage for a long time, but the nation never deemed their service to be worthy of more than the national minimum wage. Will these essential workers be honored with better wages and working conditions when this crisis has ended?

We do not seem united when Andrew Cuomo said during one of his daily news briefings about the impact of COVID-19 in his state, "It always seems that the poorest people end up paying the highest price. Why is that?"[11] Why, indeed? This is the richest nation on earth in terms of economic capacity, technological capacity, medical research and resources capacity, higher education capacity, and military capacity. Nevertheless, we remain a nation deeply divided along lines of race, region, and religion, and especially along lines of resources. Poverty is one of the great evils gripping our nation despite its great wealth. Like the opening of *A Tale of Two Cities* by Charles Dickens, it is the best of times for some Americans and the worst of times for others.

We have not seemed united when a simple thing like wearing a mask or face covering, which has the ability to slow the transmission of COVID-19, is resisted by some states, no doubt following the example of President Trump and Vice President Mike Pence, who regularly appeared in public without some sort of mask. Trump seemed concerned about how he would look while wearing a mask.[12] Pence seemed most concerned about doing whatever Trump wanted him to say or to do. Neither seemed to understand that wearing a mask is an act of mutual concern for one's self and one's neighbors. By wearing a mask, we are less likely to transmit the virus as we speak, and we are less likely to be infected by the virus as we breathe. This simple act has been called for by the medical experts and researchers trying to control the spread of COVID-19, but some people have placed their individual liberty over the common good of the country.

The church has not seemed united as we faced an interesting theological issue as a result of the COVID-19 pandemic. Do we keep our churches open and invite people to continue gathering in large numbers without concern for the spread of this disease, or do we close our doors and move our worship services online in the interest of public health and safety? Many continued to meet in person, even in states where the governor had issued orders not to do so. In some instances, those gatherings resulted in increased rates of infection. However, some persons deemed churches as essential services and insisted that they remain open.

Meanwhile, other churches decided to suspend in-person gatherings and move to virtual services using Zoom, YouTube, Facebook Live, and various forms of teleconferencing. Once again, necessity is the mother of invention. Churches found ways to hold worship services, Bible studies, funerals, weddings, congregational meetings, and fundraisers, and to stay in touch with sick and shut-in members without having to leave home. Upon my retirement as president of Colgate Rochester Crozer

Divinity School, I was asked to serve as interim pastor at Antioch Baptist Church in Cleveland, where I had formerly served as senior pastor from 1987–2011. I began that assignment in May 2020, preaching on a regular basis and hosting a Friday morning Bible class. However, I have not yet set foot inside the church building. I tape my sermons at home on Thursday morning. I send them to the cell phone of a video technician who blends them together with music and visual images. I lead a Zoom prayer conference on Sunday mornings from 10:30 to 10:45. Then at 11:00 a.m. I go to the church website to tune into the worship service to listen to myself preaching a sermon I had recorded days earlier. Given the size of our congregation relative to our seating capacity, I am not sure how or when we will ever meet together again in the sanctuary given the fact that COVID-19 may continue to require us to maintain social distancing. And given the fact that I am now seventy-one-years old and have preexisting respiratory conditions that make me vulnerable to infection, I may never return to the church during my interim assignment.

One thing is certain, no one should return to church because Trump has ordered or invited them to do so. It was astounding to hear Trump say that he hoped to see "packed churches on Easter" when COVID-19 was running rampant through the country.[13] He later said that churches should reopen in May without offering any clear guidance on how such a thing could safely be done.[14] Needless to say, our church did not follow his directive. Quite to the contrary, I wondered who gave our non-church-going President the idea that he could order churches to reopen? How does a man who has never shown any interest in religion or church life suddenly decide it is time for other people to return to church buildings that are not prepared to receive large numbers of people in the midst of the COVID-19 pandemic?

I did not hear Trump say that he was going to attend church services when the doors were reopened. To my knowledge he has not attended a church service since he issued his decree that churches should reopen. Of course, there was the one occasion when he stood in front of St. John Episcopal Church in Washington, DC, holding up a Bible.[15] That event happened only after he used National Guard troops equipped with tear gas and rubber bullets to clear a path to the church during a Black Lives Matter rally following the murder of George Floyd by a police officer in Minneapolis.[16] Trump neither entered that church to pray nor read from that Bible to console the nation. He just used the sacred text of Christians around the world as a photo opportunity.

In so many different ways, this virus has served to highlight the inequities in our United States. We know what damage it has done to human bodies. The question is, how much damage has it done to our union? We are discovering that every day.

Notes

1. Michael D. Shear and Sarah Mervosh, "Trump Encourages Protest Against Governors Who Have Imposed Virus Restrictions," *New York Times*, April 17, 2020, https://www.nytimes.com/2020/04/17/us/politics/trump-coronavirus-gov ernors.html.

2. Veronica Stracqualursi, "Michigan Closes State Capitol as Protesters Gather Against Stay-at-Home Order," CNN, May 14, 2020, https://www.cnn.com/2020/05/14/politics/michigan-state-capitol-protests/index.html.

3. Lateshia Beachum, et al., "State and City Leaders in U.S. Respond to Coronavirus Surge with New Rule and Dire Warnings," *Washington Post*, June 22, 2020, https://www.washingtonpost.com/nation/2020/06/22/coronavirus-live-updates-us/.

4. "COVID-19 Fueling Anti-Asian Racism and Xenophobia Worldwide," Human Rights Watch, May 12, 2020, https://www.hrw.org/news/2020/05/12/covid-19-fueling-anti-asian-racism-and-xenophobia-worldwide.

5. Nausheen Husain and Cecelia Reyes, "Before data showed Chicago blacks dying at higher rates, communities of color knew recovery from COVID-19" *Chicago Tribune*, April 21, 2020, https://www.chicagotribune.com/coron avirus/ct-coronavirus-chicago-health-disparities-data-20200410-rf7lmmvgur fwxpxiatebsozwsu-story.html.

6. Elvia Diaz, "Why is Coronavirus Killing So Many Black Americans?" *Arizona Republic*, April 9, 2020, https://www.redding.com/story/opinion/2020/04/09/why-coronavirus-killing-more-black-americans-because-they-poor-col umn/2973649001/.

7. Nausheen Husain and Cecelia Reyes, "Before data showed Chicago blacks dying at higher rates, communities of color knew recovery from COVID-19" *Chicago Tribune*, April 21, 2020, https://www.chicagotribune.com/coron avirus/ct-coronavirus-chicago-health-disparities-data-20200410-rf7lmmvgur fwxpxiatebsozwsu-story.html.

8. Richard S. Newman, *Freedom's Prophet: Bishop Richard Allen, the AME Church, and the Black Founding Fathers* (New York: NYU Press, 2008), 85.

9. Newman, 87–88.

10. "The Plight of Essential Workers during the COVID-19 Pandemic" *The Lancet*, May 23, 2020, https://www.thelancet.com/journals/lancet/article/PIIS0140-6736(20)31200-9/fulltext.

11. "Cuomo Vows to Investigate Racial Disparities in COVID-19 Deaths: 'Why Do the Poorest People Always Pay the Highest Price?'" The Hill, April 8, 2020, https://thehill.com/homenews/state-watch/491797-cuomo-on-disproportionate-minority-covid-deaths-why-do-the-poorest.

12. Ron Elving, "What It Means When Trump Doesn't Wear A Mask," NPR, May 8, 2020, https://www.npr.org/2020/05/08/852093558/the-president-as-a-model-for-the-nation-from-toasters-and-sweaters-to-masks.

13. Sarah Pulliam Bailey, "Trump Wants 'Packed Churches' on Easter. Pastors Expect Their Doors to be Shut," *Washington Post*, March 27, 2020, https://www.washingtonpost.com/religion/2020/03/27/churches-easter-trump-closed-coronavirus-services/.

14. Peter Baker, "Firing a Salvo in Culture Wars, Trump Pushes for Churches to Reopen," *New York Times*, May 22, 2020, https://www.nytimes.com/2020/05/22/us/politics/trump-churches-coronavirus.html.

15. Elizabeth Bruenig, "The Last Temptation of Trump," *New York Times*, June 2, 2020, https://www.nytimes.com/2020/06/02/opinion/trump-bible-speech-st-johns-church.html.

16. Jonathan Allen, Dartunorro Clark, and Rebecca Shabad, "Police, National Guard Clash with Protesters to Clear Streets before Trump Photo Op," NBC News, June 1, 2020, https://www.nbcnews.com/politics/politics-news/after-night-significant-damage-d-c-mayor-bowser-imposes-earlier-n1221126.

17

Earth's Health, Our Health: A Spirituality of Ecology amid a Global Pandemic

Elmo Familiaran

Most days, even as I go about my routine activities, I spend a good amount of time reflecting on the zeitgeist that each day presents. As I write this essay, I find myself quarantined at home in the midst of the immanence of two ubiquitous themes: the COVID-19 pandemic and the celebration of Earth Day on April 22, 2020, with its emphasis this year on climate action.

Science and theology have always coexisted in a comfortable and familiar relationship in my personal and spiritual journey. I was a community health nurse in the Philippines, headed to medical school, before I experienced a dramatic call to ministry. That admixture of academic disciplines has always informed my understanding of the world. As I was contemplating how the themes of Earth Day and the COVID-19 pandemic might be linked to each other, I was led to the premise that the emergence of the novel coronavirus is directly linked to how we relate to the planet and God's creation.

The primary biblical text that reminded me of this interrelationship is Leviticus 25, which deals with the liturgical concepts of the Sabbath Year and the Year of Jubilee. This narrative came easily to me as descriptive of the biblical claim that the physical and spiritual realms of life are aspects of the same reality. This theme is implied in all the levels of the various provisions for the sacred observance of the holy day. The command to lay the ground fallow on the seventh year as a Sabbath, and on the fiftieth year as a Year of Jubilee, underscores one of the most central assumptions of the biblical tradition which is that creation belongs to God.

> "...the land is mine; with me you are but aliens and tenants" (Leviticus 25:23)

This understanding is diametrically opposed to the dominant western and capitalistic understanding of the individual's natural right to unlimited private property, the philosophical underpinnings of which were articulated by the seventeenth century English philosopher, John Locke, in his *Second Treatise of Government*. Whether Locke intended it or not, his ideas invariably led to the formulation of political and economic theories that lent credence to imperialistic conquests and colonialist drives of western empires. Not unlike the outlook of its Spanish and Portuguese predecessors, it was a worldview that understood social and global interactions in terms of the dictum "finders keepers." In this worldview, the land not owned is considered "common" land. And because it is "common," it can be acquired without consent from anybody—notwithstanding whether indigenous peoples already inhabited the land.

But the concept of the Sabbath Year and the Year of Jubilee of laying the soil fallow—untilled and untouched—as an offering to God, is to mediate, at least liturgically, the reality that "the earth is the LORD's" (Psalm 24:1). The practical provisions governing the observance of these holy events are striking: It called for the liberation of slaves and the return of property to its rightful owners. It called for justice in economics by allowing the nearest relative of someone to redeem back land which, by force of poverty, had to be sold. It was a time to sound the trumpet and proclaim liberty to all the inhabitants of the land. The economic and ethical implications of the holy observance no doubt were aimed at preventing the accumulation of property in the hands of the few in order to forestall the creation of oppressive socioeconomic relationships. But a greater reality, in my mind, is implied in the narrative in its expressed intrusion of morality into economics.

"For it is a jubilee; it shall be holy for you." (Leviticus 25:12)

The discharge of the soil and of the earth is linked to the reverence of the divine. Indeed, the way we interact with our physical world is diagnostic of our spiritual state of being. It is clear in the text that the struggle to care for the integrity of our creation cannot be waged and sustained apart from the struggle for justice amongst people, because the faithful stewardship of the earth and its resources necessarily issue forth in the just reordering of human relationships. Conversely, justice-making in the community of peoples—in its economics and in its politics—issues forth in concrete reverential acts towards creation and nature.

The coronavirus pandemic has revealed incontrovertible evidence that human behavior directly affects the health of the environment. The quarantine life that ensued around the world withheld human activity in unprecedented ways in modern history. As a consequence, the withdrawal of human presence in the environment revealed some startling consequences in nature. As humans sheltered in place, and by extension curtailed their activities, we saw the level of particulates in the air above major urban areas like Manila, Los Angeles, Chicago, New York, and New Delhi, to name just a few, recede, giving way to stark before-and-after photos of the difference in the air quality above these cities. On May 14, 2020, a new study led by researchers at the Yale School of Public Health and published in the journal *Lancet Planetary Health*, found that China's countrywide ban on traffic mobility from February 10 to March 14 greatly limited automobile emissions and sharply reduced the country's often severe air pollution.[1] A report from mid-March disclosed that Italy's country-wide quarantine, resulting in the drastic reduction of boat traffic on the canal, had turned Venice's usually dark, murky waterways noticeably more clear—so much so that jellyfish could be seen swimming in the waters of the canal.[2]

Biblically, justice and a spirituality of ecology are linked to each other in one ecosystem, a unitary vision that has been easily lost in the marauding march of materialistic hyper-development of industry and the insatiable appetite for corporate profit. In other words, Scripture views the amoral exploitation and cruelty inflicted upon the earth and its people as acts based upon an atheistic worldview.

The very nature of spirituality, which presupposes the governance of the divine, is a perspective which is inherently supportive of the goals of justice making and the struggle to maintain ecological integrity. In 1990, twenty-three internationally respected scientists led by Carl Sagan and Hans Bethe, both renowned American astrophysicists and astronomers, issued *An Appeal for Joint Commitment in Science and Religion* which said in part:

> As scientists, many of us have had profound experiences of awe and reverence before the universe. We understand that what is regarded as sacred is more likely to be treated with care and respect. Our planetary home should be so regarded. Efforts to safeguard and cherish the environment need to be infused with a vision of the sacred.[3]

These scientists expressed their conviction that science and religion have vital roles to play in changing human behavior and, by extension, the way humans relate to nature. They asserted that religious communities make important contributions to questions of peace, human rights, and social justice. I find it very interesting that I hear this vision of the inner unity between science and nature more from scientists than from the people I know in the field of religion.

Science has taught us that microorganisms are also integral parts of nature. Viruses and bacteria are living things found everywhere on earth where there is life. In fact, viruses, which are smaller than most bacteria, are the most numerous of all life forms. And as nature would have it, all living things on earth inhabit a given ecosystem where they are supposed to coexist in balanced mutuality with each other.

But humans have long breached these ecosystems in their insatiable, avaricious, and reckless pursuit of their own survival through the rampant deforestation, destruction of habitats, and environmental pollution to make way for their own acquisitive and expansionist objectives. As if these were not enough, rapacious economics have led to horrific mass exploitation of food sources in nature through overfishing, hunting, the superstitious consumption of wild meat, and artificial mass domestication of animals outside of their natural habitats, thereby disrupting inviolably the ecological balance that they heretofore contributed to and needed in the maintenance of homeostasis of their ecosystems. Corporate greed and hyper-development have displaced entire human communities, causing mass movements of peoples seeking to settle in new, unfamiliar surroundings, and making them vulnerable hosts to new pathogens against which they do not yet have any degree of immunity.

In these ecological disruptions, viruses and bacteria that have been locked away by nature in their own ecosystems are invariably unleashed. Once their natural barriers are breached, they cross species and find new hosts among humans. The virus causing COVID-19 is called "novel" because it is new to humanity. Human beings do not yet have community immunity to guard against it. When western empires invaded and colonized indigenous peoples, they breached their community immunity by introducing new, "novel" pathogens that the ecosystem of those native peoples had never encountered before. It caused widespread epidemics, and in some cases it wiped out entire civilizations.

God created nature and pronounced it good. The inner unity and beauty of nature coheres in the harmonious place that each living organism inhabits in an ecosystem. The common theme that weaves through the Creation story in Scripture is that each member of nature has been granted a designated place—on land, sea, air, and the cosmos. God made it so that humans and nature can coexist, but God gave humans the greater responsibility of being the caretaker, the steward, of God's handiwork. A closer look at the text is quite informative.

As Jeff A. Benner notes in his ancient Hebrew word study, the commands to "subdue" and to "have dominion" over the earth, are derived from the original Hebrew words, *kavash* and *radah*, respectively.[4] *Kavash* is the verb form of the noun, *kevesh*, which literally means "a footstool," like putting one's foot on the neck of one's defeated enemy. And so, to "put a kavash" on something figuratively means to bring someone or something into submission. Our common understanding of to "have dominion" over another is to tyrannically rule over subjects.

But the verb *radah* belongs to a word group that conveys the meanings of to descend, to go down, to wander around—to rule by going down and walking among one's subjects as an equal. And so scholars have long interpreted the existence of the words *kavash* and *radah* in the same verse to mean that humans are to rule over the animals and the fruits of the earth not as a tyrant or a dictator, but as a benevolent leader acting out of profound gratitude to the bounty that Creator God has granted to them. God, therefore, calls humanity to have a relationship with creation that reveres the work of the Creator, so that nature not only provides for the needs of humanity but also teaches humanity about the unity of all of life.

As stewards of the earth, we are to watch over nature and enjoy its abundance. To "subdue" and "have dominion" over the earth does not mean to plunder it, nor to take from it more than it can give. By violating such a simple rule of nature, humans have been directly instrumental in the extinction of many species. To be stewards of the earth, in the biblical sense, means that we are to be mindful of the fragility of nature and to revere its finiteness. In doing so, we become mindful of our own fragility and revere our own finiteness.

The Mozuku seaweed, which grows around the island of Okinawa, is one of the most sought-after delicacies in Japan.[5] Okinawans have followed for centuries the traditional Japanese wisdom of *satoumi* (pronounced, sato-umi), which essentially means, "when you work harmoniously with nature, the sea will always provide." In the clear, shallow coastal waters around the island are vast underwater grids of natural fiber rope, spread around in sectors that provide the platform on which the prized seaweed grows naturally. It is then harvested manually by a scuba diver based on flat-bottomed boats, using a handheld hydraulic-powered vacuum hose that gently sucks the seaweed onto the boat above, barely disturbing the ecosystem below the water surface. Okinawans have cultivated this food source in its own natural habitat and have developed carefully scheduled harvesting methods that ensure sustainability. This philosophy has guided these marine farmers to relate with ecosystems in a harmonious way for prolonged periods of time. And in that sustained symbiotic relationship where nature is treated with reverence, new landscapes were formed whereupon humans and nature can coexist harmoniously. They practice *kavash* and *radah*.

The COVID-19 pandemic has revealed that we are all part of a complex, fragile, and tenuous planetary web of interconnectedness. This pandemic has shattered our human delusions that our primary reason for existence is to reign over and exploit nature, that we are to not care about the integrity of the earth because we are disembodied from the rest of creation, and that our actions do not have consequences that affect us.

In the ecological and social upheaval that the earth is going through right now because of the pandemic, we see the deconstruction of long-held assumptions of how we have organized ourselves as a society. It has acutely exposed the injustices of a global economy whose wealth and resources are controlled to benefit only a privileged few. It has exposed the plight of the poor, the less privileged, and the subsistence worker and the scandal of their lack of access to basic healthcare and living wages.

We are also discovering the limits of the digital age as organizations and religious communities struggle to find alternative ways of organizing within the constraints of the massive social distancing requirements of health guidelines. While the internet has made us more connected, it also reveals that it can make us more isolated.

We cannot go back to normal, if normality is understood as the way things used to be and the usual ways we behaved towards each other and nature. Scientists will soon disclose with certainty the source or the host of the COVID-19 virus. And when that source is identified, we will also learn how that source jumped species and entered the human community. With that knowledge, human behavior will and must inviolably change. The behavior towards nature, and towards each other, that led to the pandemic can no longer be repeated, even with the advent of a vaccine.

The tragedy of this pandemic is revealing so much darkness in our society, in our economy, and in our politics. But is has also revealed so much heretofore unseen ways of humanity's capacity for goodness, as peoples and strangers reach out in new ways to help and comfort each other. The church now has a powerful platform to reclaim one of its ascribed and ancient voices, granted to it as a people of God. The church must reassert its voice in society as a passionate advocate of the care of the earth, not merely as a political cause or as a programmatic adjunct to its mission. Rather, the church must be a frontline advocate for the care of the earth as a matter of fundamental biblical and spiritual responsibility.

The earth's health is our health.

To Learn More

Darwin, Charles. *The Origin of Species*. (London: J. Murray, 1859).

Paul, Lain. *Science, Theology, and Einstein*. (Oxford: Oxford University Press, 1982).

Moltmann, Jürgen. *God in Creation: The Gifford Lectures 1984–1985*. (Minneapolis, MN: Fortress Press, 1993).

Teilhard de Chardin, Pierre. *The Phenomenon of Man*. (New York: Harper & Brothers, 1959).

Notes

1. Michael Greenwood, "In China, Strict Quarantine Improves Air Quality and Prevents Thousands of Premature Deaths," Yale School of Medicine, May 14, 2020, https://medicine.yale.edu/news-article/24721/.

2. Catherine Clifford, "The Water in Venice, Italy's Canals is Running Clear Amid the COVID-19 Lockdown—Take a Look," CNBD, March 18, 2020, https://www.cnbc.com/2020/03/18/photos-water-in-venice-italys-canals-clear-amid-covid-19-lockdown.html

3. "Preserving and Cherishing the Earth: An Appeal for Joint Commitment in Science and Religion," *Global Forum, Moscow, National Religious Partnership for the Environment*, January 1990, http://earthrenewal.org/Open_letter_to_the_religious_.htm.

4. Jeff A. Benner, "Subdue," Ancient Hebrew Research Center, https://www.ancient-hebrew.org/definition/subdue.htm.

5. BBC Earth, "Sucking Up Seaweed?" YouTube video, July 22, 2016, https://www.youtube.com/watch?reload=9&v=deZja5i_B3o.

18
Deaf Ministry in Times of Crisis—Signs of Hope

Lori Buck

The twenty-first century church should be an inclusive and welcoming place, where all people can perceive the gospel as it is taught and preached. It is the right thing to do, good for your community and not that difficult to accomplish. Churches must respond to God's call and invite persons who are Deaf and hard of hearing (DHH) into the fold. If you enjoy worshiping at your church, others will too. God's people are blessed to become a blessing to others. If you are blessed by your worship experience, share it and pass it on to others.

There is a need for Deaf ministry in churches to effect changes to include DHH persons in participation, leadership, and all aspects of worship and fellowship. Many pastors are not aware of the numerous persons with gifts and talents yet untapped within their church and community. Their gifts and talents will benefit Deaf ministry. DHH persons, their family members, friends, co-workers, and neighbors are in your church. Congregants should be asked to participate in Deaf ministry.

Imagine this: A visitor walks into your church, ushers greet and seat the visitor, and the entire church sings and simultaneously signs a song in unison. There's not a frown to be found; warmth, peace, and smiles abound. The visitor enjoys the hospitality, praise, and worship as never before. The visitor leaves after the service ends, meets her friends to grab a bite, and shares her experience. The next Sunday, the visitor brings one of those friends and places an envelope in the offering plate. Later, a trustee opens the envelope and finds the following handwritten poem and note:

> I walked into this place
> A smile was on each face
> Not done with glue or paste

People seemed so chaste
Perhaps they had what it takes
There seemed to be so much faith
And they looked so safe

I wasn't paralyzed by limitation
As there was open communication
Quite meaningful inspiration
It was more than an inclination
For that ecstatic exhilaration

Because love was in the air
Hope was in their hearts
Nothing was keeping us apart
Signs were in their hands
And I could finally understand!

I'm a college student who happens to be Deaf. A friend told me about this church. I loved seeing the entire church "signing" that song together. It was a like a little piece of heaven. I wanted to connect with this place. It felt like a big, loving family.

The trustee shares the poem with the other trustees and presents it to the pastor. The following week, the pastor shares the poem with the congregation during the welcoming of visitors. The pastor asks whether the author of the poem is present and would care to stand. She stands. People clap loudly, hugging and welcoming her. Now, she is really part of a larger family.

If every church had an outreach ministry, the community would be a better place for both the hearing and the DHH communities. No one knows if a person is Deaf or hard of hearing unless they actually attempt to communicate. Members with warm smiles and signs of communication and love are highly valued treasures. Are there signs of love and buried treasure in your church? Fulfill the need for Deaf ministry now—it matters!

Impact of the COVID-19 Pandemic on the Deaf Community

Life as we knew was upended because of the coronavirus pandemic. This crisis endangered countless lives and affected everyone in some way—economically, emotionally, mentally, physically, ecologically, or spiritually. Arguably one of the worst pandemics the world has faced, it caused more American deaths than the Vietnam War and more job loss than the Great Depression, and it affected business more than the 2008 financial crisis.

Business closures and shelter-in-place restrictions mandated video conferencing and online meetings, mandatory work from home when and where possible, and contactless banking. Education was disrupted and only available online from elementary grades through college. Graduation ceremonies were canceled. With the onset of the pandemic came daily updates from government and public health officials regarding the extent of its spread and impact.

Other than the 1918 flu pandemic, which killed one-third of the population at that time, COVID-19 was the worst pandemic the world ever faced. It impacted and changed how we think, clean, work, learn, dine, socialize, travel, exercise, and communicate. With daily updates on the spread of the virus heard on the radio, television, and the internet, the pandemic also raised concerns about how we communicate important information with the people who are Deaf and hard of hearing.

Accessibility to Information

Persons who are DHH are more reliant on visual communication and need access to all communication regarding a pandemic in their language—sign language. Sign language is the most important method of communication in the Deaf world.[1] It is used as both a simple and a complex method of communicating to convey ideas, thoughts, feelings, and information. American Sign Language (ASL), with its own syntax, grammar structure, idioms, and vocabulary, is the native language of most people in the Deaf community in the United States. ASL is independent of the English language. ASL provides a cultural linguistic identity for persons who are Deaf and offers pride, language, instruction, role models, and more that cannot be experienced elsewhere.[2] For these reasons, the DHH community defines itself as a linguistic minority culture as opposed to a disabled or handicapped community.

How aware are you of Deaf individuals next door, at the grocery store, in college, graduate school, work, church, hospitals, and everywhere else? Did you know that one out of every hundred persons in America is DHH; therefore, there are more than thirty million persons with hearing loss in the United States? Half a million people are born Deaf and unable to understand speech through the ear. Other Deaf people hear well enough to carry on a conversation in spoken English and to use the telephone.[3]

Ministry Needs of the Deaf Community in Times of Crisis

During the crisis, safety for members, staff, and visitors became paramount. As a result of the stay-at-home order, congregations could not gather or meet inside church buildings. Churches had to use technology to minister, connect, and remain relevant. All ministries had to meet online or telephonically. In some cases, this required church staff and members to quickly learn how to use these technologies.

When churches reopen, members may have to eliminate traditional greetings like shaking hands, hugging, and holy kissing on the cheek. We may not be able to fist bump without gloves or elbow bump without long sleeves. We may have to greet and show love with signs and facial expressions instead.

This crisis presents the Christian community new opportunities to establish, maintain, and strengthen relationships with the Deaf community. It may also provide an opportunity to reach many who previously had no exposure to the church. Some of the approaches to consider include:

■ Conducting Deaf ministry activities such as meetings, bible discussions, game nights and fellowships using videoconferencing platforms, (e.g., Zoom). In this setting, everyone communicates in ASL.

■ Allowing Deaf individuals to experience all of the church's livestreamed content by hosting videoconferencing meetings in which the livestreamed event is shared alongside an interpreter or interpreting team. This will allow Deaf members the same access to livestreamed events as their hearing counterparts.

■ Adding an interpreter to all prerecorded content. For church events that are prerecorded, the recordings would be provided to the interpreting team. A member of the team would then record themselves interpreting the content. The interpreted video would be sent back to the audio/visual team to sync. When the content is synced, the interpreter and person teaching/ preaching are side by side.

■ In addition to these activities, we cannot forget the power of one-on-one connection. It is essential that Deaf ministries are intentional about staying connected. One approach might be to assign each member a buddy. A buddy is someone you connect with periodically by email, text, video message, or some other technique. Other approaches might be to activate a phone or text message tree or assign ministry leaders to individuals they are responsible for staying connected with.

DHH persons must be included in *all* of the ministry planning. They are the experts regarding their needs and expectations.

Signs of Hope for Ministry to the Deaf Community in Crisis

Accessibility: Is Your Church Deaf-Friendly?

As found by Gate Communications, 93% of the Deaf in America have no contact with a church. Fewer than 2% of the Deaf have an active relationship with Jesus. The Deaf community is considered the third- or fourth-largest unreached group with the gospel of Christ. Less than three hundred individuals are serving in full time Deaf ministry worldwide. In 2005, forty-two out of sixty-five Deaf churches in America did not have a pastor, and less than 5% of churches in the United States offer Deaf outreach.[4]

Does your church have a Deaf ministry? It should not be a matter of whether to have a Deaf ministry, but when to have a Deaf ministry.[5] What would your life be like without sound? A hearing person's life without sound is equivalent to a DHH person's life without ASL. Consider what having a Deaf ministry in your church would mean. It would mean that DHH can choose your church as their house of worship. Have you considered that churches with a Deaf ministry serve more people in the community than those who do not? How glorious it would be if all of God's children, Deaf and hearing persons, could dwell in unity at the church of their choosing and worship with sign language and signs and wonders.

While there are numerous challenges to establishing the ministry, there are resources that provide guidance regarding church organization and structure, human resources, and spiritual development. For hearing persons, learning ASL is an important step in establishing significant social relationships with those who are deaf and hard of hearing. Community colleges often offer courses in ASL. Churches should consider enhancing their online presence and virtual programming. For the church with limited resources, there are a few internet companies that will allow an organization to build a webpage without charge or hosting fees. For members who do not own laptops or desktop computers, the public computers at a local library are a good way to keep in touch or search for information. A loaner laptop program could be implemented with a donation of as little as two laptops from members or companies nearby. Law firms are particularly good resources for donations of laptops or desktop computers since they update or replace technology every few years and often look for ways to give back to the community.

Awareness: Building the Deaf Ministry Team

It will take a collaborative effort of both DHH and hearing persons to bring about transformation, new direction, and focus in the ministry and church community. Progress takes teamwork, passion and action. It also takes love. "Let love be your highest goal! (1 Corinthians 14:1 NLT).

A healthy ministry functions best with a strong team. Jesus formed a team for the purpose of ministry. We should do likewise. It takes a team to create, develop, and sustain a ministry. Deaf ministry should be developed as a team of members working together for the common goals of its members and ministry. The team concept is essential if the ministry is to thrive, and increase in efficiency, and effectiveness.

Pray, fellowship, and build upon a good foundation as a team. Learn to build bridges of friendship one moment and one person at a time. Great things can be achieved when members of a ministry collaborate.[6]

Inclusion: Designing a Deaf Ministry Strategy

Once you have a team in place, it's time to launch the ministry. Strive to emulate the master strategist, Jesus. The Deaf ministry should endeavor to love, empower, enlighten, reach, teach, equip, and evangelize DHH persons to experience significant spiritual growth and meaningful involvement in ministry and decision-making in the church. Every church member needs to share the vision of participating in ministry or becoming a ministry leader in order to fulfill the Great Commission of Jesus Christ (Matthew 28:19), which is to go and make disciples of all nations. Jesus' plan was to take a group of people and prepare them to represent him in the world. The group of disciples that Jesus prepared for ministry became the leaders of the first century church—its establishment, organization, and outreach to the most remote parts of their society. Because of Jesus' plan, we are following him and reading their writings two thousand years later. What a plan! Not only must there be a plan, there must be preparation in order to implement the plan.[7]

Summary

Where would we be without technology? In this pandemic, it seems we cannot communicate with anyone without technology. Numerous DHH children have hearing parents and siblings that either do not know ASL or do not sign well. Therefore, without technology, stay-at-home orders would be devastating because that would mean limited contact with family, friends, and the outside world. Family and friends that we love and care about are the most important parts of our lives as they encourage and brighten our days in myriad ways. However, during a stay-at-home order you're isolated. At a time when you need to be around people you love the most, you're separated and sheltering in place. How much more difficult is it to be single, live alone, and be deaf? Communication is also important to good mental health.

We need to design a more inclusive society once the pandemic is contained. Let us together shape a "new normal" where communication access for DHH people is standard. Since we're in this together, let's allow the crisis to bring out the best in us and care enough to shape the future with Deaf ministry.

Life is bittersweet, filled with good times and bad. Enjoy and value the good and prepare for the bad. Always have hope for the future. When experiencing a bitter battle, why not seize the opportunity to reshape a better future for ourselves and others? Why not use this present crisis to plan and prepare for greater access for the Deaf and hard of hearing? Our efforts can encourage hope and change a life.

Crises can prompt us to focus more on our spiritual beliefs. Let our actions be influenced by love. Crises can increase feelings of anxiety, fear, loneliness, and frustration, a sense of loss and hopelessness. However, our faith compels and challenges us to embrace others. The DHH community is an untapped resource whose voice yearns to be heard. In or out of a crisis, let us spread hope. As Emily Dickinson wrote,

> "Hope" is the thing with feathers –
> That perches in the soul –
> And sings the tune without the words –
> And never stops - at all.[8]

Let us together commit to learn to speak the language of love, faith, and hope with signs and words.

Notes

1. Harlan Lane, Robert Hoffmeister, Ben Bahan, *A Journey into the Deaf-World* (San Diego, CA: DawnSignPress, 1996) 162–165.

2. Lane et al., 161.

3. Carol Padden and Tom Humphries, *Inside Deaf Culture* (Cambridge, MA: Harvard University Press, 2006) 1–2.

4. "General Statistics Regarding Deafness," Gate Communications, https://www.gatecommunications.org/statistics.

5. Portions of this chapter adapted from Lori Buck, *Signs of Love: A Guide for Deaf Ministry* (Valley Forge, PA: Judson Press, 2014).

6. Buck, 60.

7. Buck, 61.

8. Emily Dickinson, "254," *The Complete Poems of Emily Dickinson* (New York: Little, Brown and Company, 1961), 116.

About the Contributors

Lori Buck is the author of *Signs of Love: A Guide for Deaf Ministry* and founder of SWS Consulting. Buck is an ordained minister, has presented at various religious interpreters' workshops, and has consulted with churches to develop deaf ministries. Lori has earned an MTS and DMin from Wesley Theological Seminary in Washington, DC.

Matthew Crebbin, an ordained minister in the United Church of Christ, has been senior minister at the Newtown Congregational Church, UCC, since 2007 and was a clergy first responder during the mass shooting at Sandy Hook Elementary School on December 14, 2012. He holds a BA in Legal Studies from the University of California at Berkeley as well as a MDiv from Andover Newton Theological School. He has been a leader in promoting gun safety policies, finding other means locally and nationally to reduce gun violence in all communities, and helping people of faith to understand the challenges and opportunities of ministering in the midst of trauma and disasters.

Elmo Familiaran is an adjunct faculty member at Palmer Theological Seminary. He is ordained in the American Baptist Churches USA, and is a thirty-nine-year veteran in pastoral ministry, ecumenical and cross-cultural engagement, and executive leadership in both national and regional denominational settings. A graduate of Northern Seminary and the New York Theological Seminary, he is the co-author of *No Greater Love: Triumph and Sacrifice of American Baptist Missionaries During WW II Philippines, and the Martyrdom in Hopevale.*

Angela Gorrell is assistant professor of Practical Theology at Baylor University's Truett Seminary and the author of *Always On: Practicing Faith in a New Media Landscape*. She is ordained in the Mennonite Church

USA and holds a PhD in Practical Theology from Fuller Theological Seminary. Her guides for Christian leaders who want inspiration for taking their ministry online are available at angelagorrell.com

Jeffrey Haggray is executive director of American Baptist Home Mission Societies and Chief Executive Officer of Judson Press, based in King of Prussia, Pennsylvania. He also leads ABHMS' mission in the area of Public Witness and Advocacy and serves on several non-profit boards, including Bread for the World, Church World Service, Baptist Joint Committee for Religious Liberty, and Andover Newton Seminary at Yale.

Debora Jackson is director of operations of All Girls Allowed, a faith-based non-profit organization dedicated to restoring life, value, and dignity to women and girls through education and empowerment. Formerly the director of Lifelong Learning at Yale Divinity School and executive director of the Ministers Council of the American Baptist Churches USA, Dr. Jackson has also served as senior pastor of the First Baptist Church in Needham, MA, and in numerous corporate leadership positions. She is the author of the award-winning title, *Spiritual Practices for Effective Leadership: 7Rs of Sanctuary for Pastors* (Judson Press, 2015), and *Meant for Good: Fundamentals of Womanist Leadership* (Judson Press, 2019).

Greg Johnson is senior pastor of Cornerstone Community Church in Endicott, New York. He is a recognized ordained clergy of American Baptist Churches USA and is ecclesiastically endorsed by American Baptist Home Mission Society Chaplaincy and Specialized Ministry. He serves as the protestant chaplain for the Greater Binghamton Health Center in Binghamton, New York. Johnson the author of the book, *Merging with Grace: A Healthy Transformation* and has authored numerous articles.

Rachael B. Lawrence, an ordained American Baptist pastor, is copastor at Second Baptist Church of Suffield, CT, and Executive Director of KinderSpirit Inc. In addition to a PhD from the University of Massachusetts Amherst, she holds degrees from the University of Akron and Heidelberg College. She is a frequent contributor to *The Christian Citizen*.

Greg Mamula is the associate executive minister for the American Baptist Churches of Nebraska. Mamula is the author of *Table Life: An Invitation to Everyday Discipleship* (Judson Press, 2021). He coedited the book *Conflict Management and the Apostle Paul* with Scot McKnight (2018). He also writes for *Word & Way*, *The Christian Citizen*, and *Good Faith Media*.

Margaret Marcuson helps pastors bring their best to their ministry without giving it all away, so they can have a greater impact and find more satisfaction. She is an American Baptist minister and can be found at margaretmarcuson.com.

Marvin A. McMickle is the retired president of Colgate Rochester Crozer Divinity School. He is pastor emeritus of Antioch Baptist Church in Cleveland, Ohio, and professor emeritus of Preaching at Ashland Theological Seminary in Ashland, Ohio. He is the author of seventeen books, and his forthcoming book by Judson Press, *Let the Oppressed Go Free: Reflections on Fifty Years of Liberation Theologies*, will be released in the spring of 2021.

Lauren Lisa Ng is director of Leadership Empowerment at the American Baptist Home Mission Societies where she works with innovative and entrepreneurial models of ministry and the emerging leaders who pursue them. Ordained in the American Baptist Churches USA, she earned her MDiv from the American Baptist Seminary of the West and is currently pursuing the DMin in Creative Leadership at Central Baptist Theological Seminary.

About the Contributors

Naomi Kohatsu Paget, is an FBI chaplain and crisis interventionist. She serves California Southern Baptist Disaster Relief and is an adjunct professor at Gateway Seminary and Denver Seminary. She is the national chairperson for the Emotional & Spiritual Care Committee of the National Voluntary Organizations Active in Disasters.

Curtis Ramsey-Lucas is editor of *The Christian Citizen*, a digital-first publication of American Baptist Home Mission Societies. He is editor of *The Christian Citizen Weekly* e-newsletter and host of the "Justice. Mercy. Faith." podcast. His articles have appeared in *The Washington Post, Religion News Service, Sojourners, Baptist News Global,* and *Good Faith Media.*

Susan Sparks is the senior pastor of the historic Madison Avenue Baptist Church in New York City, a professional comedian, an award-winning nationally syndicated columnist, and the author of multiple books. Her work has been featured in *O (The Oprah) Magazine,* the *New York Times,* and on such networks as ABC, CNN, CBS, and the History Channel.

Marilyn Turner-Triplett heads the Healing and Transforming Communities ministries of American Baptist Home Mission Societies. Ordained in the American Baptist Churches USA, she is the author of *Justice for Rizpah's Children: Radical Responses to Childhood Poverty* (Judson Press, 2019). She serves as an associate minister of Bethlehem Baptist Church, Penllyn, Pennsylvania, and holds an honorary doctorate from Alderson Broaddus University.

Cassandra Carkuff Williams, an ordained American Baptist Minister, serves as the National Coordinator for Discipleship Ministries with the American Baptist Home Mission Societies. She holds a ThM in Biblical Studies from Union Presbyterian Seminary and an EdD from Presbyterian School of Christian Education, and she is author of *Learning the*

Way: Reclaiming Wisdom from the Earliest Christian Communities (Alban, 2009).

Michael Woolf is a Doctor of Theology candidate at Harvard University and the senior minister of Lake Street Church of Evanston, Illinois. He is an ordained American Baptist minister and a scholar of the Sanctuary Movement of the 1980s. He is currently writing his dissertation, "Sanctuary and Subjectivity," on the experiences of recipients of sanctuary.

John Zehring served United Church of Christ congregations as senior pastor in Massachusetts, Rhode Island, and Maine. Prior to parish ministry, he served as a vice president and teacher at colleges, universities, and a theological seminary. He is the author of recent Judson Press books on church growth and on stewardship. He graduated from Eastern University and holds graduate degrees from Princeton Theological Seminary, Rider University, and the Earlham School of Religion.